Christmas 18

Sue Ped.

have a very happy

Christmas

enjoy your culinary

pursuits !

Linda Mike x x x

DARINA ALLEN
SIMPLY DELICIOUS
The Classic Collection

DARINA ALLEN
SIMPLY DELICIOUS
The Classic Collection

100 timeless, tried & tested recipes

Photography by Peter Cassidy

Kyle Books

To the memory of Myrtle Allen, my lifelong inspiration

An Hachette UK Company
www.hachette.co.uk

First published in Great Britain in 2018 by
Kyle Books, an imprint of Kyle Cathie Ltd
Carmelite House, 50 Victoria Embankment, London EC4Y 0DZ
www.kylebooks.co.uk

ISBN: 978 0 857835 123

Publisher: Joanna Copestick
Editor: Vicky Orchard
Design: Jane Humphrey
Photography: Peter Cassidy
Food styling: Lizzie Harris
Props styling: Agathe Gits
Production: Nic Jones and Gemma John

A Cataloguing in Publication record for this
title is available from the British Library

Printed and bound in Italy

10 9 8 7 6 5 4 3 2 1

RECIPE SYMBOLS

❄ Freezes perfectly for 2–3 months
but use sooner rather than later.

contents

Introduction

Early in 1987, 'a knock came to the door' as we say in Ireland, and the postman delivered a letter that in some ways was to change the course of the rest of my life. It was from the Controller of Programmes at RTÉ, our national television station, and contained a proposal to Myrtle Allen and I for a pilot for a cookery series. It was terrifically exciting, tempting in many ways, but also beyond scary… I had never seen a television camera in my life and had absolutely no idea how to go about making a television programme. I tossed the proposal backwards and forwards in my head, scared I would make a total fool of myself, yet excited at the prospect. After much toing and froing I decided it would be easier to live with the series not being a huge success than with the eternal question of 'What if…?'

We filmed the pilot in August 1987 and RTÉ commissioned the first series in July 1988, to be filmed that September. The original plan was to publish the recipes in the weekly RTÉ Guide but I was concerned that we would have endless phone calls when people mislaid it. So, despite having no idea how to go about writing a cookbook either, I proposed that I do just that. The producer Colette Farmer was concerned that there wouldn't be enough recipes, but the Ballymaloe Cookery School had been operating since 1983, so we already had a growing repertoire of dishes – so no problem there. Gill & Macmillan agreed to publish the cookbook in paperback, but what to call it…The name Darina Allen meant nothing at that time, so after much discussion with the crew, *Simply Delicious* was proposed. Apparently, I had repeated these two words regularly and it seemed to reflect the food that I loved to cook and was so anxious to share – how easy it was to make simple and delicious food with beautiful, fresh local produce.

The first programme was to be aired on Monday 13th March 1989 at 8pm. My director Colette Farmer was also production assistant and later a producer of the *Late Late Show* and was famous in her own right as the face behind the command 'Roll it there Colette', when Gay Byrne would show a previously recorded piece during an interview. She understandably had Gay's ear so he agreed to have me on as a guest on his Saturday night show, I was never so terrified before or since, but survived. Gay could be unpredictable, even provocative, but he introduced me enthusiastically to the Irish people and I was launched.

After the first few programmes people poured into the shops to buy the little 78-page *Simply Delicious* paperback. For many, it was the first cookbook they ever owned, the recipes well-tested for the Ballymaloe Cookery School worked, so as the Gill & Macmillan representative put it one night after a book signing, the book was selling in 'telephone numbers' and shops quickly ran out of copies. It went into a second printing immediately and there was a paper shortage, so for several of the eight weeks the programme was on air there wasn't a copy of *Simply Delicious* to be had in the country. Furthermore, the success was fuelled by another unlikely element. RTÉ didn't anticipate the appeal of this new cookery series and ran it opposite *Coronation Street*. This was at a time when most houses would have been proud to own just one television and long before any form of playback, so there was many a family 'fracas' about which programme to watch. Viewers wrote to RTÉ and rang into chat shows to complain that it was causing 'strife' within the family. The repeat was rescheduled…

Simply Delicious went on to make Irish publishing history, topping the best sellers for months in a row and selling more copies than any previously published cookbook in Ireland: 115,000 copies in the first year of publication. I went on to do a further six *Simply Delicious* books to accompany a series of the same name.

I've often been told that 'dog-eared' copies of these books are treasured possessions in many households and have in many cases been passed on to the next generation. Since then I've gone on to publish a further sixteen cookbooks. The *Simply Delicious* books have been out of print for many years but people regularly ask where they can find a copy of one or another, so I'm delighted to be republishing this collection of 100 classic recipes from *Simply Delicious 1* and *2* and *Simply Delicious Vegetables*.

Choosing the recipes was a fascinating experience, so many have stood the test of time and are still perennial favourites. Some we have tweaked over the past 30 years or added more contemporary garnishes or complementary spices as the range of ingredients available has expanded considerably in the time since the recipes were first published.

Many of our happiest childhood memories are connected to food. I hope you will enjoy this selection of recipes. For me it's such a joy to know that for many, these simply delicious dishes have become treasured favourites to share with family and friends around the table. And I'm hoping that many of these time-honoured recipes will still be relished and enjoyed in 30 years' time…

soups & starters

WINTER CELERY SOUP
with Cashel Blue & toasted hazelnuts

Serves 8–10

Celery gets a bad rap but at Ballymaloe we cook it in lots of exciting ways – I love this wintery soup, light and delicious garnished with creamy crumbly blue cheese and some toasted hazelnuts.

600g celery, finely chopped
45g salted butter
150g potatoes, peeled and cut into 5mm dice
150g onions, chopped
850ml homemade chicken stock
150–300ml creamy milk
salt and freshly ground black pepper

For the garnish
a few tablespoons whipped cream
2 tablespoons Cashel Blue or Crozier Blue cheese, crumbled
2 tablespoons hazelnuts, skinned, toasted and coarsely chopped
sprigs of chervil or flat-leaf parsley

Use a potato peeler to remove the strings from the outside stalks of the celery and save to use in stock.

Melt the butter in a heavy-bottomed saucepan. When it foams, add the potatoes, onions and celery; toss in the butter until evenly coated. Season with salt and freshly ground pepper. Cover with a paper lid (to keep in the steam) and the saucepan lid and sweat over a gentle heat for about 10 minutes until the vegetables are soft but not coloured. Add the chicken stock and simmer for 10–12 minutes until the celery is fully cooked. Liquidise the soup, add a little more creamy milk or stock to thin to the required consistency. Season to taste.

Serve the soup piping hot with a little blob of whipped cream on top. Sprinkle with the crumbled Cashel Blue, coarsley chopped hazelnuts and sprigs of chervil or flat-leaf parsley.

VARIATION

⁓ *For a vegetarian version* substitute vegetable stock for the chicken stock and for a vegan option use extra virgin olive oil instead of butter and omit the milk, cream and cheese.

WATERCRESS SOUP

Serves 6–8

This soup has been a favourite on the menu at Ballymaloe House since it opened in 1964. Watercress contains large amounts of vitamins K, C and A, some vitamins E and B6. It also contains iron, calcium, manganese, potassium, thiamine, magnesium and phosphorus and is a valuable source of nutrients. Wild watercress has more depth of flavour than the cultivated version, so see if you can find some to use in this recipe.

45g salted butter

150g potatoes, peeled and chopped

110g onions, chopped

900ml homemade chicken stock, vegetable stock
   or water, boiling

300ml creamy milk, boiling

225g chopped watercress,
   coarse stalks removed

salt and freshly ground black pepper

Melt the butter in a heavy-bottomed saucepan, when it foams, add the potatoes and onions and toss them until well coated. Sprinkle with salt and freshly ground pepper. Cover with a paper lid and the lid of the saucepan and sweat over a gentle heat for 10 minutes.

When the vegetables are almost soft but not coloured add the boiling stock and milk. (It is essential to boil the stock and milk before adding, otherwise the enzymes in the watercress may cause the milk to curdle.)

Return to the boil and cook until the potatoes and onions are fully cooked. Add the freshly chopped watercress, return to the boil, and cook with the lid off for 4–5 minutes until the watercress is just cooked. Be careful not to overcook the soup or it will lose its fresh green colour. Serve as is or purée the soup in a liquidiser. Season to taste.

VARIATION

For a vegetarian version use vegetable stock and for a vegan version substitute extra virgin olive oil for the butter and use extra vegetable stock instead of milk.

MUSHROOM SOUP

Serves 8–9

This is a super quick soup to make and best made with flat mushrooms, as they have so much more flavour than the button variety. You can also substitute wild mushrooms *Agaricus campestris*, in season. Give them a quick wash under the tap. Trim the roots if necessary, though it's better to leave the roots in the ground if you are foraging yourself.

The soup base of this recipe (without the stock) is a great way to preserve a glut of field mushrooms. It freezes perfectly for several months. To use, just defrost, add the stock and milk and then bring to the boil for 3–4 minutes. Season to taste before serving.

45g salted butter

115g onions, finely chopped

450g flat mushrooms

25g plain flour

600ml homemade chicken stock, boiling

600ml whole milk, boiling

dash of cream (optional)

salt and freshly ground black pepper

Melt the butter in a saucepan over a gentle heat. Toss the onions in it, cover with a paper lid and sweat until soft and fully cooked.

Meanwhile, chop the mushrooms very finely. It's best to hand-chop the mushrooms but if you don't have time to chop the mushrooms very finely, just slice them and then pulse the cooked soup in a liquidiser for a second or two. Be careful not to overdo it, as the soup should be chunky.

Add the mushrooms to the saucepan and cook over a high heat for 5–6 minutes. Now, stir in the flour, cook over a low heat for 2–3 minutes, season with salt and freshly ground pepper.

Add the boiling stock and milk gradually, stirring all the time. Increase the heat and bring to the boil. Taste and add a dash of cream if necessary. Serve immediately or reheat later.

VARIATION

For a vegetarian version substitute vegetable stock for the chicken stock, and for a vegan version use extra virgin olive oil to replace the butter. Instead of milk and cream use all stock or substitute soya or almond milk.

ONION & THYME LEAF SOUP

Serves 6

❄

This silky, flavoursome soup is so much more than the sum of its parts. Serve it in one of two ways, depending on your mood. You may want to purée it to a smooth texture or just ladle it directly into a wide soup bowl with all the chunky bits intact. It's irresistible scattered with fresh thyme leaves and flowers in season.

45g salted butter

450g onions, chopped

225g potatoes, peeled and chopped

2 teaspoons fresh thyme leaves

1 litre homemade chicken or vegetable stock,
   boiling

150ml cream or creamy milk

salt and freshly ground black pepper

whipped cream (optional), to garnish

fresh thyme leaves and thyme or chive flowers,
   to garnish

Melt the butter in a heavy-bottomed saucepan. As soon as it foams, add the onions and potatoes and stir until they are well coated with butter. Add the thyme leaves and season with salt and freshly ground pepper. Cover with a paper lid and the lid of the saucepan and sweat over a low heat for about 10 minutes. The potatoes and onions should be soft but not coloured. Add the hot chicken stock, bring to the boil and simmer for 5–8 minutes until the onions and potatoes are cooked. Liquidise the soup and add a little cream or creamy milk to taste. Season to taste.

Serve in soup bowls or in a soup tureen garnished with a blob of softly whipped cream, if you wish. Sprinkle with thyme leaves and thyme or chive flowers to garnish.

VARIATION

For a vegetarian version substitute vegetable stock for the chicken stock, and for a vegan option use extra virgin olive oil instead of butter and omit the cream and milk.

SPRING CABBAGE SOUP

Serves 6

It doesn't seem to occur to many people to use cabbage for soup, yet of all the soups I make, the flavour of cabbage soup surprises most – it is unexpectedly delicious. I use Greyhound or Hispi cabbage but crinkly Savoy cabbage works brilliantly later in the year.

55g salted butter

115g onions, chopped

130g potatoes, peeled and diced

850ml homemade light chicken stock, boiling

250g spring cabbage leaves, shredded
   and chopped (stalks removed)

50–125ml cream or creamy milk

salt and freshly ground black pepper

chorizo crumbs or Gremolata (page 84), to garnish
   (optional)

Melt the butter in a heavy-bottomed saucepan. When it foams, add the onions and potatoes, toss them in the butter until well coated. Sprinkle with salt and freshly ground pepper. Cover with a paper lid and the lid of the saucepan and sweat over a gentle heat for 10 minutes until soft but not coloured. Add the hot stock and boil until the potatoes are tender. Add the cabbage and cook uncovered for 4–5 minutes until the cabbage is just cooked. Keep the lid off to preserve the bright green colour. Do not overcook or the vegetables will lose both their fresh flavour and colour.

Purée the soup in a liquidiser or blender. Season to taste. Add the cream or creamy milk before serving. Serve alone or with a sprinkling of chorizo crumbs or gremolata over the top, if you wish.

VARIATION

For a vegetarian version substitute vegetable stock for the chicken stock and use Gremolata instead the chorizo crumbs to garnish. For a vegan option use extra virgin olive oil instead of butter and omit the cream or creamy milk.

VINE-RIPENED TOMATO & SPEARMINT SOUP

Serves 5

Tomato soup is to soup what apple tart is to desserts – top of the list of all-time favourites. The marvellous thing about this recipe is that you can easily vary it in so many different ways, making it almost seem like a different soup each time. It's best to use a tomato purée made from vine-ripened tomatoes in season. However, good-quality tinned tomatoes also produce a really good result, but because they are rather more acidic than fresh tomatoes you need lots more sugar.

There are many varieties of mint in the herb garden but spearmint is the most versatile and has the cleanest, freshest taste. Try to find the type that has shiny rather than furry leaves. Basil or coriander can also be substituted for spearmint with delicious results.

15g salted butter

110g onions, finely chopped

750ml homemade tomato purée (see right)
    or 2 x 400g tins of chopped
    tomatoes, liquidised and sieved

250ml béchamel sauce (page 00)

250ml homemade chicken or vegetable stock

2 tablespoons freshly chopped spearmint,
    plus extra leaves to garnish

1–2 tablespoons granulated sugar

120ml cream (optional)

a slick of softly whipped cream, to serve

salt and freshly ground black pepper

For the tomato purée

900g very ripe tomatoes

1 small onion, chopped

good pinch of granulated sugar

good pinch of salt

a few twists of black pepper

To make the tomato purée, cut the tomatoes into quarters and put into a stainless steel saucepan with the onion, sugar, salt and freshly ground pepper. Cook over a gentle heat until the tomatoes are soft (no water is needed). Put through the fine blade of a mouli legumes or a nylon sieve. Leave to cool completely then chill or freeze.

Melt the butter in a medium saucepan over a gentle heat, when it foams add the onions, toss, and cover with a paper lid and the lid of the saucepan. Cook for 5–6 minutes until soft but not coloured. Add the homemade tomato purée or the puréed tinned tomatoes, the béchamel sauce and chicken stock. Bring to the boil, add the chopped mint, season with salt, freshly ground pepper and sugar if you are using tinned tomatoes – otherwise just a pinch. Bring to the boil and simmer for a few minutes. Liquidise, taste, dilute further if necessary with extra chicken stock.

Return to the boil, season to taste and serve with the addition of a little cream if desired. Garnish with a swirl of whipped cream and some freshly shredded spearmint. Like most soups, this one can be refrigerated for 3–4 days and it reheats very well.

WINTER LEEK & POTATO SOUP

Serves 6–8

The classic winter soup loved by everyone, from tiny tots to elders. Once again this soup can be served either with the chunks of vegetables intact or puréed. A tablespoon of finely sliced buttered leeks served in the centre of this soup makes a more substantial version.

50g salted butter

450g potatoes, peeled and cut into 5mm dice

110g onions, cut into 5mm dice

450g white parts of the leeks, finely sliced (save the green tops for another soup or vegetable stock)

850ml–1.2 litres light homemade chicken stock, boiling

100ml whipping cream, plus extra to garnish

150ml whole milk

sea salt and freshly ground black pepper

finely chopped chives, to garnish

Melt the butter in a heavy-bottomed saucepan, when it foams, add the potatoes, onions and leeks, turn them in the butter until well coated. Season well, sprinkle with salt and freshly ground pepper and toss again. Cover with a paper lid and the saucepan lid. Sweat over a gentle heat for 10 minutes or until the vegetables are soft but not coloured.

Discard the paper lid. Add 850ml hot stock, return to the boil and simmer until the vegetables are just cooked. Do not overcook or the soup will lose its fresh flavour.

Liquidise the soup until smooth and silky, taste and adjust the seasoning, if necessary. Add cream and milk to taste. You may need to add extra stock if you prefer a thinner soup. Garnish with a swirl of cream and some finely chopped fresh chives.

VARIATIONS

⌐ *Green Leek & Potato Soup* Use the green parts of the leeks as well as the more delicate blanched root ends. The soup will have a stronger flavour but will also be super-delicious.

⌐ *Vichyssoise* Serve chilled in small bowls with extra cream and a little sprinkling of chives and a few fresh chive flowers sprinkled over the top in season.

⌐ *For a vegetarian version* substitute vegetable stock for the chicken stock, and for a vegan option use extra virgin olive oil instead of the butter and omit the cream and milk.

SWEDE & BACON SOUP with parsley oil

Serves 6–8

I love swede, an inexpensive, super-versatile vegetable with lots of flavour and one that's often forgotten. This soup is an example of how it can sing. A little diced chorizo or some chorizo crumbs mixed with some chopped parsley is also delicious sprinkled on top.

1 tablespoon sunflower oil

150g rindless streaky bacon, cut into 1cm dice

110g onions, chopped

110g potatoes, peeled and diced

350g swede, peeled and cut into 7mm dice

900ml homemade chicken stock

cream or creamy milk, to taste

salt and freshly ground black pepper

For the parsley oil

50g freshly chopped flat-leaf parsley

50ml extra virgin olive oil

For the garnish

freshly ground black pepper

fried diced bacon

croutons

First make the parsley oil. Whizz the parsley with the olive oil until smooth and green.

Next make the soup. Heat the oil in a saucepan, add the bacon and cook over a gentle heat until crisp and golden. Remove to a plate with a slotted spoon and set aside.

Toss the onions, potatoes and swede in the oil. Season with salt and freshly ground pepper. Cover with a paper lid to keep in the steam and sweat over a gentle heat for about 10 minutes until soft but not coloured. Add the stock, bring to the boil and simmer for 10–15 minutes until the vegetables are fully cooked. Liquidise, taste and add a little cream or creamy milk and some extra seasoning if necessary.

Serve with a drizzle of parsley oil, a grind of black pepper and a mixture of crispy bacon and croutons sprinkled on top.

VARIATION

For a vegetarian version use vegetable stock instead of chicken stock and omit the bacon. For a vegan option omit the cream or creamy milk as well.

GREEN PEA SOUP with fresh mint cream

This soup has the quintessential flavour of summer. If you have beautiful fresh peas, use the pods to make a vegetable stock and use that as a basis for the soup. Having said that, best-quality frozen peas also make a delicious soup. Either way, be careful not to overcook.

This soup may also be served chilled in smaller portions. It can be enjoyed unblended but the flavour is more intense when puréed. To serve, put a few fresh peas and pea shoots into wide soup bowls. Put the soup in a jug – each guest then pours the soup into their bowl themselves.

25g streaky bacon or lean ham

15g salted butter

2 spring onions, green and white parts, chopped

outside leaves of a head of lettuce, shredded

a sprig of fresh mint, plus some freshly
   chopped mint, to garnish

1.2 litres light homemade chicken or
   vegetable stock or water, boiling

pinch of granulated sugar

675g podded peas, fresh or frozen

2 tablespoons whipping cream

sea salt and freshly ground black pepper

whipped cream, to garnish

Cut the bacon into very fine shreds. Melt the butter and sweat the bacon for about 5 minutes, then add the spring onions and cook for a further 1–2 minutes. Next add the lettuce, mint and boiling chicken stock or water. Season with sugar, salt and pepper. Return to the boil with the lid off, add the peas and cook for 3–4 minutes or until the peas are just tender.

Liquidise and add a little cream to taste. Serve hot or chilled with a blob of whipped cream and some freshly chopped mint.

If this soup is made ahead, reheat uncovered and serve immediately. It will lose its fresh taste and bright lively colour if it sits in a bain-marie or simmers at length in a pot.

VARIATIONS

Pea & Bacon or Chorizo Soup Add a few tiny crispy lardons of bacon or chorizo as a garnish.

For a vegetarian version use vegetable stock and omit the ham, bacon or chorizo. For a vegan version, use extra virgin olive oil instead of butter and omit the cream too.

POTATO & FRESH HERB SOUP

Serves 6

❄

Most people have potatoes and onions in the house even if the cupboards are otherwise bare, so can make this simply delicious soup at a moment's notice. While the vegetables are sweating, pop a few white soda scones or Cheddar cheese scones into the oven to really impress your family and friends. I sometimes omit the fresh herbs and drizzle the soup with parsley or rocket pesto. Some buttered cabbage or kale stirred in before serving changes it into colcannon soup, while crispy bacon lardons or chorizo and sprigs of flat-leaf parsley transform potato soup into a 'cheffier' version.

55g salted butter

425g potatoes, peeled and cut into 75mm dice

110g onions, cut into 75mm dice

1 teaspoon salt

few grinds of freshly ground black pepper

1–2 tablespoons in total of the following fresh herbs: parsley, thyme, lemon balm and chives

900ml homemade chicken or vegetable stock, boiling

120ml creamy milk

freshly chopped herbs and chive or thyme flowers in season

Melt the butter in a heavy-bottomed saucepan. When it foams, add the potatoes and onions and toss them in the butter until well coated. Sprinkle with the salt and a few grinds of pepper. Cover with a paper lid and the lid of the saucepan. Sweat over a gentle heat for about 10 minutes.

When the vegetables are soft but not coloured add the freshly chopped herbs and hot stock and continue to cook for 3–4 minutes or until the vegetables are soft.

Purée the soup in a blender or food processor. Season to taste. Thin with creamy milk to the required consistency.

Serve sprinkled with a few freshly chopped herbs and some chive or thyme flowers in season.

VARIATION

‿ *For a vegetarian version* use vegetable stock, and for a vegan option use extra virgin olive oil instead of the butter and omit the milk.

LEBANESE COLD CUCUMBER SOUP

Serves 8–10

A cooling summer soup which can be adapted to make a little cucumber mousse ring which in turn can be topped with a variety of good things. Variations of this soup are found all over the Middle East, in Iran, Syria and Iraq. It's literally made in minutes and can be eaten immediately but I like to serve it well chilled in little bowls or glasses.

1 large cucumber, organic if possible
180ml light cream
180ml natural yogurt (unsweetened)
1 tablespoon tarragon vinegar (page 74)
1 small garlic clove, crushed

1 tablespoon finely chopped gherkins (optional)
2 tablespoons finely chopped mint
sea salt and freshly ground black pepper
sprigs of mint and dried rose petals, to garnish

Grate the cucumber on the coarsest part of the grater. Stir in all the other ingredients except the mint sprigs and rose petals. Season well. Serve chilled in small bowls garnished with a sprig of mint and a couple of dried rose petals.

VARIATION

Little Cucumber Mousse Sponge 8g powdered gelatine in 2 tablespoons of cold water in a small bowl. Put the bowl into a small saucepan of boiling water, when liquid becomes clear add a couple of tablespoons of the soup mixture and stir well. Combine with the remaining soup and pour into little glasses. I fill 100ml glasses three-quarters full. Cover for 3–4 hours or until set. Garnish with a little salad of some freshly chopped walnuts and dried rose petals.

SMOKED TROUT cucumber & horseradish cream salad

Serves 8

A simple, but delicious combination – easy to assemble. The horseradish cream cuts the richness of the trout. It is a mild horseradish sauce, but if you would like something that will really clear the sinuses, just increase the quantity of grated horseradish.

1–2 cucumbers

a sprinkle of wine vinegar

pinch of granulated sugar

1 teaspoon freshly chopped fennel or

   2 teaspoons freshly chopped fresh dill

8 fillets of smoked sea or rainbow trout salt and

freshly ground black pepper

For the horseradish cream

1½–3 tablespoons peeled and grated horseradish

2 teaspoons wine vinegar

¼ teaspoon lemon juice

¼ teaspoon mustard

3 teaspoons salt

a pinch of freshly ground black pepper

1 teaspoon granulated sugar

250ml softly whipped cream

For the garnish

salmon caviar (optional)

lemon segments

fresh dill or fennel fronds

First, make the horseradish cream. Put the grated horseradish into a bowl with the vinegar, lemon juice, mustard, salt, freshly ground pepper and sugar. Fold in the softly whipped cream, but do not overmix or the sauce will curdle. This sauce keeps for 2–3 days in the fridge and may also be served with roast beef. Cover it tightly so that it doesn't pick up flavours in the fridge.

Thinly slice the cucumbers (with peel on). Sprinkle with a few drops of vinegar and season with sugar, salt and a little freshly ground pepper and stir in some finely chopped fennel or dill.

To assemble the salad, lay a fillet or a few chunks of smoked trout on each plate. Add some cucumber salad and a dollop of fresh horseradish cream. Top with salmon caviar, if using. Garnish with lemon segments or some fresh dill and fennel.

CRUDITÉS WITH AIOLI

This is one of my favourite starters – small helpings of very crisp vegetables with a good garlicky homemade aioli. It fulfils all my criteria for a first course: plates of crudités look tempting, taste delicious and provided the helpings are small, are not too filling. Better still, it's actually good for you – so you can feel very virtuous instead of feeling pangs of guilt!

Another bonus is that I've discovered children love crudités. They even love aioli provided they don't hear some grown-up saying how much they dislike garlic. You can feel happy to see your children polishing off plates of raw vegetables for supper, that are really quick to prepare and bursting with vitamins and minerals.

Crudités can be a perfect first course for winter or summer, but to be really delicious you must choose very crisp and fresh organic vegetables. Cut the vegetables into bite-sized pieces so they can be picked up easily. There's no need for cutlery because they can be eaten with fingers. The Italian version of crudités is called pinzimonio – just serve them with a bowl of the very best extra virgin olive oil you can find instead of the aioli.

Use as many of the following vegetables as are in season:

tomatoes quartered, or whole with the calyx on
   if they are freshly picked
purple sprouting broccoli, broken (not cut)
   into florets
calabrese (green sprouting broccoli),
   broken into florettes
cauliflower, broken into florettes
French beans or mangetout
fresh asparagus
baby carrots, or larger carrots cut into 5cm sticks
cucumber, cut into 5cm sticks
courgette blossoms
tiny spring onions, trimmed
red cabbage, cut into strips
celery, cut into 5cm sticks
chicory
radicchio
fennel, thinly sliced

red or yellow pepper, cut into 5cm strips,
   seeds removed
very fresh Brussels sprouts, cut into halves
   or quarters
whole radishes, with green tops left on
parsley, finely chopped
thyme, finely chopped
chives, finely chopped
sprigs of watercress

For the aioli

2 organic, free-range egg yolks
pinch of English mustard powder or ¼ teaspoon
   French mustard
1–4 garlic cloves, depending on size
¼ teaspoon salt
1 dessertspoon white wine vinegar
250ml sunflower or olive oil
   or a mixture – I use 150ml sunflower oil
    and 75ml extra virgin olive oil
2 teaspoons freshly chopped flat-leaf parsley
freshly ground black pepper

continued overleaf

First make the aioli. Put the egg yolks into a Pyrex bowl with the mustard, finely crushed garlic, salt and white wine vinegar (save the whites to make meringues). Put the oil into a measuring jug with a good pouring spout. Take a whisk in one hand and the oil in the other and drip the oil onto the egg yolks, drop by drop, whisking at the same time. Within a minute you will notice that the mixture is beginning to thicken. When this happens you can add the oil a little faster, but don't get too cheeky or it will suddenly curdle because the egg yolks can only absorb the oil at a certain pace. Taste and add a little more seasoning and vinegar if necessary.

If the aioli curdles it will suddenly become quite thin, and if left sitting the oil will start to float to the top of the sauce. If this happens you can quite easily rectify the situation by putting another egg yolk or 1–2 tablespoons of boiling water into a clean bowl, then whisk in the curdled aioli, ½ teaspoon at a time until it re-emulsifies. Add the chopped parsley and season to taste.

A typical plate of crudités might include the following: a baby carrot or 4 sticks of carrot, 2 leaves of chicory, radicchio or fennel, 2 sticks of cucumber, 1 whole radish with a little green leaf left on, 1 tiny tomato or 2 quarters, 1 Brussels sprout cut in quarters, sprouting broccoli or romanesco florets, a sprig of watercress and a little pile of chopped fresh herbs.

Wash and prepare the vegetables. Arrange on individual white side plates in contrasting colours, with a little blob or bowl of aioli in the centre.

Alternatively, prepare a large dish or basket for the centre of the table. Arrange little mounds of each vegetable in contrasting colours. Put a bowl of aioli in the centre and guests can help themselves. Instead of serving the aioli in a bowl, you could make an edible container by cutting a slice off the top of a tomato and hollowing out the seeds. Alternatively, cut a 4cm round of cucumber and hollow out the centre with a melon baller or a teaspoon. Then fill or pipe the aioli into the tomato or cucumber. Arrange the aioli in the centre of the plate of crudités. It's a bit 1950s but delicious nevertheless.

VARIATION

Suitable for vegetarians For a vegan version substitute olive oil for the aioli, as in pinzimonio. Pinzimonio is a Tuscan appetiser. Fresh, crunchy vegetables are dipped into a bowl of the finest Tuscan extra virgin olive oil - fresh fennel, asparagus, baby carrots, celery sticks... simple but delicious.

RILLETTES OF FRESH & SMOKED SALMON

Serves 16–20

This is a terrific standby recipe that can be tarted up in all sorts of ways or simply slathered on hot thin toast or crusty bread. The texture of this pâté should be coarse and slightly stringy – it should resemble that of pork rillettes, where the meat is torn into shreds with forks rather than blended. Don't be spooked by the amount of butter you use – you're not going to eat it all yourself!

375g salted butter, softened
350g smoked wild or organic salmon
1 tablespoon water
350g freshly-cooked wild salmon
a good grating of nutmeg
lemon juice, to taste

freshly chopped fennel (optional)
salt and freshly ground black pepper
clarified butter (page 185 – optional)
dill or fennel fronds and flowers, to garnish
hot, thin sourdough toast, to serve

Melt 25g butter in a small saucepan; add the smoked salmon and the water. Cover and cook for 3–4 minutes or until it no longer looks opaque. Leave it to get quite cold.

Cream the remaining butter in a bowl. With two forks, shred the fresh and smoked salmon and mix well together. Add to the soft butter still using a fork (do not use a food processor). Season with salt and freshly ground pepper and lots of freshly grated nutmeg. Taste and add lemon juice as necessary, and a little freshly chopped fennel if you have it.

Serve in individual pots or in a pottery terrine. Cover with a layer of clarified butter if you wish. They keep perfectly in the fridge for 5–6 days provided they are sealed with clarified butter.

Garnish with dill or fennel fronds and flowers in season. To serve, toast or chargrill a slice of sourdough bread and spread with some rillette mixture. Salmon rillettes may be frozen but use within a few weeks.

VARIATIONS

Salmon Rillettes with Cucumber Slices Cut 2 cucumbers into 5mm-thick slices. Spoon a blob of pâté onto each cucumber slice. Garnish with sprigs of chervil and fennel, dill, chive or wild garlic flowers in season. Arrange three slices on a plate with a little salad in the centre or serve as a starter or canapé.

Extra Posh Salmon Rillettes Line 12–16 moulds 5cm in diameter, 2.5cm deep, with clingfilm. Put a slice of smoked salmon into each mould. Fill the moulds with the rillettes; fold the ends of the smoked salmon over the rillettes to cover. Cover with clingfilm and chill for at least one hour. Serve with cucumber pickle.

MUSHROOM CROSTINI with rocket & Parmesan

Serves 2

Who doesn't love mushrooms on toast? Virtually all fungi are delicious served in this way, so this can be very humble or very exotic depending on the variety chosen. Nowadays I prefer to char the bread on a hot grill pan, then rub with a clove of garlic, but the original version is also delicious.

2 slices of sourdough or a large
   good-quality baguette
extra virgin olive oil
butter, garlic butter or majoram butter, for frying
4–6 breakfast flats, Portobello,
   or large oyster mushrooms

freshly chopped marjoram
2 garlic cloves
rocket leaves
freshly shaved Parmesan cheese,
   Parmigiano Reggiano if possible
salt and freshly ground black pepper

Char the sourdough on a hot grill pan or heat 2.5cm of olive oil in a frying pan until just below smoking point. Fry the pieces of bread one at a time, whip them out just as soon as they become golden. Drain on kitchen paper and keep warm. (The oil may be strained and used again for another purpose.)

Heat a little olive oil or olive oil and butter in a frying pan. Remove the stalks from the mushrooms and place them skin-side down on the pan in a single layer, put a little dot of butter into each one or better still use garlic or marjoram butter. (This is made quite simply by mixing some chopped garlic and parsley or some annual marjoram into a little butter.) Alternatively, sprinkle with freshly chopped marjoram and a clove of crushed garlic if you like. Season with salt and freshly ground pepper.

Cook first on one side (the length of time will depend on the size of the mushroom: it could take anything from 3–6 minutes), then turn over as soon as you notice that the gills are covered with droplets of juice. Cook on the other side until tender.

Meanwhile, rub the surface of the warm crostini with a cut garlic clove, put on two hot plates. Arrange a few fresh rocket leaves on each one, top with overlapping mushrooms. Sprinkle on a few more rocket leaves and a little freshly slivered or grated Parmesan cheese and serve immediately. If there are any buttery juices in the pan, spoon every drop over the mushrooms for extra deliciousness.

VARIATION

Suitable for vegetarians if you use a vegetarian alternative to the Parmesan. For a vegan version, omit the butter and cheese.

PRAWNS OR SHRIMP ON BROWN BREAD

with homemade mayonnaise

Serves 4

Don't dismiss this very simple starter. Spanking fresh prawns or shrimp are wonderful served on good brown bread with a homemade mayonnaise. If using shrimp, use a little of the coral for garnish. Alternatively, serve the freshly cooked prawns or shrimp still in their shells with brown bread and homemade mayonnaise.

175g prawn tails or shrimp, freshly cooked

4 slices brown bread, thinly sliced, crusts removed
    and buttered

4 leaves butterhead, oakleaf or lollo rosso lettuce

3 tablespoons homemade mayonnaise (page 146)

4 lemon segments and sprigs of watercress,
    flat-leaf parsley, fennel or garden cress,
    to garnish

Peel the fat, freshly cooked prawn tails or shrimp. Put a slice of buttered bread on a plate, arrange 1 or 2 lettuce leaves on top, and place 5–6 prawns on the lettuce. Pipe a coil of homemade mayonnaise on the prawns, just enough so the proportion of each ingredient looks right. Garnish with lemon segments and sprigs of watercress, flat-leaf parsley, fennel or garden cress.

VARIATION

Prawn or Shrimp Canapés Tiny versions of these on rounds or squares of bread make a delicious canapé to go with drinks.

BALLYMALOE CHICKEN LIVER PÂTÉ
with crostini

Serves 10–12

My goodness, how this recipe stood the test of time – it has been our house pâté at Ballymaloe since the opening of the restaurant in 1964! Served in many different ways: its success depends upon being generous with good Irish butter. Sherry can be delicious instead of brandy occasionally. It is essential to cover chicken liver pâté with a layer of clarified or even just melted butter, otherwise the pâté will oxidise and become bitter in taste and grey in colour.

225g fresh organic chicken livers
200–300g salted butter (depending on how
   strong the chicken livers are)
1 large garlic clove, crushed

1 teaspoon fresh thyme leaves
2 tablespoons brandy
freshly ground black pepper
clarified butter (page 185), to seal the top

Wash the chicken livers in cold water and remove any membrane or green tinged bits. Dry on kitchen paper.

Melt a little butter in a frying pan; when the butter foams add the livers and cook over a gentle heat. Be careful not to overcook them or the outsides will get crusty; all trace of pink should be gone. Add the crushed garlic and thyme leaves to the pan, stir and then deglaze the pan with brandy, allow to flame or reduce for 2–3 minutes. Scrape everything with a spatula into a food processor. Purée for a few seconds. Leave to cool.

Add 225g butter, cut into cubes and purée until smooth. Season to taste.

This pâté should taste fairly mild and be quite smooth in texture. Serve in little ramekins, little glass pots, or in one large terrine. Tap on the worktop to knock out any air bubbles. Spoon a little clarified butter over the top of the pâté to seal.

Pâté may also be formed into a roll, wrapped in clingfilm or greaseproof paper and refrigerated. Later the paper is removed and the roll of pâté can be decorated with finely chopped herbs and herb flowers.

Serve with crostini, toast or sourdough. This pâté will keep for 4–5 days in the fridge.

VARIATION

Chicken Liver Pâté with Pedro Ximénez Jelly Soak 1 sheet of gelatine in cold water for 4–5 minutes, when soft discard the water. Warm 150ml Pedro Ximénez gently in a saucepan, add the gelatine and allow to melt. Cool, then spoon over the top of each ramekin of pâté instead of the butter..

WARM BACON & AVOCADO SALAD
with walnut oil dressing

Serves 6

Warm salads were all the rage in the late eighties and early nineties, but they have stood the test of time and still make a delicious starter or light lunch – this simple combination was, and still is, one of my favourites. The larger the selection of your salad leaves the more interesting the salad will be.

a selection of lettuces and salad leaves, such as butterhead, iceberg, endive, radicchio, trevisano, watercress, salad burnet

175g streaky bacon, in one piece, unsmoked or lightly smoked

clarified butter (page 185), or mixture of butter and oil, for frying

4 slices of good white bread

sunflower or olive oil, for frying

1 large or 2 small avocados

18 fresh walnut halves, to garnish (optional)

For the walnut oil dressing

3 tablespoons walnut oil or 2 tablespoons walnut oil and 1 tablespoon sunflower oil, mixed

1 tablespoon Chardonnay wine vinegar

1 teaspoon freshly chopped chives

1 teaspoon freshly chopped flat-leaf parsley

salt and freshly ground black pepper

Wash and dry the salad leaves and tear them into bite-sized pieces. Put into a bowl, cover and chill until needed.

Cut the rind off the piece of bacon and discard. Cut the bacon into 5mm cubes. Fry until golden in clarified butter or a mixture of butter and oil. Drain on kitchen paper.

To make the croutons, first cut the crusts off the bread, then cut into 5mm strips and into exact cubes. Heat the sunflower or olive oil in a frying pan, it should be at least 2cm deep and almost smoking. Add the croutons to the hot oil. Stir once or twice, they will colour almost immediately. Put a sieve over a Pyrex or stainless steel bowl. When the croutons are golden brown, pour the oil and croutons into the sieve. Drain the croutons on kitchen paper. Croutons may be made several hours ahead or even a day.

Make the walnut oil dressing by whisking the liquid ingredients together then add the chopped herbs and season with salt and freshly ground pepper.

Halve the avocado, remove the stone, peel and cut into 1cm dice.

To serve, toss the salad leaves in just enough dressing to make the leaves glisten. Add the crisp, warm croutons and the diced avocado. Toss gently and divide the salad between six plates. Re-fry the bacon in a little olive oil in a hot pan until crisp and golden, then scatter the hot bacon over the salad. Garnish with a few fresh walnut halves, if you wish. Serve immediately.

ONION BHAJIS with tomato & chilli relish

Serves 4
as a starter

Bhajis are street food in India, eaten immediately hot and crisp from the karahi in a newspaper package – here we serve them as a first course or small plate with a tomato and chilli sauce. Cheap, cheerful and delicious!

110g plain flour

2 teaspoons baking powder

1 teaspoon chilli powder or smoked paprika

2 organic eggs, beaten

150ml water

4 onions, thinly sliced in rings

1 tablespoon freshly snipped chives or coriander

oil, for deep frying

salt and freshly ground black pepper

For the tomato & chilli relish

25g green chillies, deseeded and chopped,
   or 2–3 depending on size

1 red pepper, deseeded and cut into 5mm dice

½ x 400g can chopped tomatoes

1 garlic clove, crushed

1 dessertspoon caster sugar

1 dessertspoon soft brown sugar

1 tablespoon white wine vinegar

2 tablespoons water

First make the relish. Put the chillies, pepper, tomatoes and garlic into a stainless steel saucepan with the sugars, vinegar and water. Season and simmer for 10 minutes until reduced by half.

Sift the flour, baking powder and chilli powder into a bowl. Make a well in the centre, add the eggs, then gradually add in the water and mix to make a smooth batter. Stir in the thinly sliced onions and chives. Season well with salt and freshly ground pepper.

Just before serving heat the oil to about 170°C. Fry dessertspoons of the batter for about 5 minutes on each side until crisp and golden, then drain on kitchen paper. Serve hot or cold with the tomato and chilli relish.

LYDIA'S TRADITIONAL IRISH SALAD

Serves 4

This simple old-fashioned salad is the sort of thing you would have had for tea on a visit to your Granny on a Sunday evening – perhaps with a slice of meat left over from the Sunday joint. It is still one of my absolute favourites. It's super delicious made with a crisp lettuce, ripe home-grown tomatoes and cucumbers, organic eggs and home-preserved beetroot. If, on the other hand, you make it with pale, battery farmed eggs, watery tomatoes, tired lettuce and cucumber and (worst of all) vinegary beetroot from a jar, you'll wonder why you bothered.

In summer we serve it as a starter in Ballymaloe House, with an old-fashioned salad dressing which would have been popular before the days of mayonnaise. It brings back happy nostalgic memories for many people. The salad dressing recipe came from Lydia Strangman, the last occupant of our house.

2 organic eggs

1 butterhead lettuce

2–4 ripe sweet tomatoes, quartered

16 slices of cucumber

4 tiny spring onions

4 sliced radishes

4 tablespoons pickled beetroot and onion

watercress sprigs

freshly chopped parsley

For Lydia Strangman's salad cream dressing

2 organic eggs

1 tablespoon soft dark brown sugar

pinch of salt

1 level teaspoon mustard powder

1 tablespoon brown malt vinegar

50–125ml double cream

Hard-boil all four eggs. Bring a small saucepan of water to the boil, gently slide in the eggs and boil two for 7 minutes so they are soft in the centre. Boil the other two eggs for 10 minutes. Strain off the hot water and cover with cold water. Peel when cold.

Next make the dressing. Cut two of the hard-boiled eggs (which you have cooked for 10 minutes) in half and sieve the yolks into a bowl. Add the sugar, a pinch of salt and the mustard. Blend in the vinegar and cream. Chop the egg whites and add some to the dressing. Keep the rest to scatter over the salad. Cover until needed.

To assemble the salads, first arrange a few lettuce leaves on each of four plates. Add a few tomato quarters, half a hard-boiled egg, a few slices of cucumber and a radish on each plate, and (preferably just before serving) add slices of pickled beetroot and onionsto each. Garnish with spring onions and watercress. Scatter with the remaining egg white (from the dressing) and some chopped parsley. Add a spoon of salad cream dressing to each plate and serve immediately, while the salad is crisp and before the beetroot starts to run. Serve the extra dressing in a large bowl.

poultry

TURKEY BAKED WITH MARJORAM

Serves 12–14

This casserole roasting technique is a totally brilliant way of cooking not only turkey, but also chicken, pheasant and guinea fowl. You'll have lots of flavourful juices as the base for a delicious sauce. This whole dish can be prepped ahead, covered and reheated. Use the turkey carcass and giblets if you have them. There are several varieties of marjoram; the one we use for this recipe is the annual sweet or knotted marjoram – *origanum majorana*.

1 x 4.5–5.4kg organic, free-range turkey
2–3 sprigs marjoram
110g salted butter, softened

4 tablespoons freshly chopped marjoram,
    plus extra to garnish
900ml single cream
salt and freshly ground black pepper

Preheat the oven to 180°C/gas mark 4.

If time allows, brine the turkey overnight, it's so worthwhile for the extra depth of flavour. The next day, drain and dry. Remove the wishbone from the neck end of the turkey for ease of carving. Also remove the fat from the vent end, season the cavity with salt and freshly ground pepper and stuff with the sprigs of fresh marjoram – there's no need for extra salt if the turkey has been brined.

Smear the breast and legs of the turkey with 55g butter. Put the turkey breast-side down into a large casserole and cook over a gentle heat for 6–8 minutes or until the skin on the breast turns golden. Turn the other way up and smear with half the chopped marjoram mixed with the remaining butter. Season with salt and freshly ground pepper. Cover with greaseproof paper and a tight-fitting lid. Cook for 2–2½ hours. Check if the turkey is cooked; the juices should be clear and there should be no trace of pink between the thigh and the breast.

Remove the turkey to a carving dish and leave to rest while the sauce is being made. De-grease the cooking juices, add the light cream, bring to the boil, taste and reduce if necessary to strengthen the flavour. Add the remaining chopped marjoram. Add the juices from the carving dish to the sauce. Season to taste.

Carve the turkey and nap with the sauce. Garnish with freshly chopped marjoram.

CHICKEN WITH MUSHROOMS & ROSEMARY

Serves 4

Soaking the chicken breasts in milk gives them a meltingly tender and moist texture. I often serve this with orzo, a pasta that looks like grains of rice, but noodles or fettuccine also work well. The flavour of rosemary varies throughout the year so start by adding half a tablespoon of freshly chopped rosemary to the sauce, taste and add more if needed.

4 free-range organic chicken breasts

milk (optional)

15g salted butter

1 small sprig of rosemary, plus extra sprigs to garnish

2 tablespoons chopped shallots or spring onions

110g mushrooms, sliced

150ml homemade chicken stock

150ml single cream

½–1 tablespoon freshly chopped rosemary

roux (page 76)

salt and freshly ground black pepper

For the orzo (optional)

200g orzo

15–25g salted butter or a drizzle of extra virgin olive oil

freshly ground black pepper

1 tablespoon freshly chopped flat-leaf parsley

Soak the chicken breasts in just enough milk to cover them for about 1 hour, then drain. Dry the chicken breasts with kitchen paper and season with salt and pepper.

Heat most of the butter in a sauté pan until foaming, put in the chicken breasts and turn them in the butter (do not brown); add a sprig of rosemary and cover with a round of greaseproof paper and the lid. Cook over a gentle heat for 5–7 minutes or until just barely cooked.

Meanwhile, sweat the shallots gently in a pan in the remaining butter – remove to a plate. Increase the heat, add the mushrooms, season with salt and freshly ground pepper and cook for 3–4 minutes. Add to the shallots and set aside.

For the orzo, bring 2–3 litres of water to a fast rolling boil and add 1½ teaspoons of salt. Sprinkle in the orzo and cook for 8–10 minutes or until just cooked. Drain, rinse under hot water, toss with a little butter or extra virgin olive oil. Season with freshly ground pepper and add some freshly chopped parsley.

When the chicken breasts are cooked remove to a plate, discard the sprig of rosemary. Add the chicken stock and cream to the saucepan with the chopped rosemary. Bring to the boil, whisk in a little roux – just enough to thicken the sauce slightly. (If the sauce is too thick, add a little chicken stock to thin to a light coating consistency.) When you are happy with the flavour and texture of the sauce, add the chicken breasts and the mushroom mixture back in, simmer for 1–2 minutes and season to taste. Serve immediately garnished with sprigs of fresh rosemary and the orzo alongside.

FARMHOUSE CHICKEN

Serves 8

A whole meal in a dish, this was, and still is, a favourite family supper in our house.
I often serve it in the big black roasting tin, on the table, family style.

1.575kg organic, free-range chicken

560g fat streaky bacon in one piece

2 tablespoons sunflower oil

seasoned plain flour

400g onions, finely sliced or chopped

340g carrots, cut into 1cm slices

approx. 2.3kg large 'old' potatoes, such as Golden Wonders or Kerr's Pinks

1.1 litres homemade chicken stock, boiling

sea salt and freshly ground black pepper

1 tablespoon freshly chopped parsley, to garnish

Preheat the oven to 230°C/gas mark 8.

Joint the chicken into 8 pieces; separate the wing joints so they will cook evenly. Cut the rind off the bacon and cut 225g into lardons and the remainder into 5mm-thick slices. If salty, blanch, refresh and dry on kitchen paper. Set the slices aside.

Heat the oil in a wide frying pan and cook the lardons until the fat begins to run and they are pale golden; transfer to a plate. Toss the chicken joints in the seasoned flour, sauté in the bacon fat and oil until golden on both sides, remove from the pan and put with the bacon. Finally toss the onions and carrots in the bacon fat for 1–2 minutes.

Peel the potatoes and slice a little less than half into 5mm rounds. Arrange a layer of potato slices on the bottom of a deep 38cm square roasting tin. Season with salt and freshly ground pepper. Top with a layer of seasoned chicken joints. Cut the remaining potatoes into 4cm-thick slices lengthways and arrange cut-side up on top of the chicken (the whole top of the dish should be covered with potato slices). Season with salt and freshly ground pepper. Pour the boiling chicken stock into the roasting tin.

Bake for about 1 hour. After 30 minutes of cooking, top with the slices of bacon so they get deliciously crisp with the potatoes. Test after 1 hour – it may take a little longer. Cover loosely with parchment paper near the end of cooking if the top is getting too brown. The vegetables will have absorbed much of the stock, but the dish should still be moist and juicy underneath the crisp potatoes and bacon slices on top. Sprinkle with chopped parsley and serve.

CASSEROLE ROAST PHEASANT

with apple & Calvados

Serves 4

This recipe comes from Valle d'Auge in Normandy in France where they have wonderful rich cream and delicious apples. Chicken or guinea fowl may also be used in this recipe. Here, I'm using the brilliant casserole roasting technique again (see page 48).

1 plump young, well hung pheasant
40g salted butter
50ml Calvados
225ml cream or 110ml cream and
    110ml homemade chicken stock
roux (optional – page 76)

2 dessert apples, such as Golden Delicious or
    Cox's Orange Pippin, peeled and cut into
    7mm dice
sea salt and freshly ground black pepper
sprigs of watercress or chervil, to garnish

Preheat the oven to 180°C/gas mark 4.

Choose a casserole, preferably oval, just large enough to fit the pheasant. Season the cavity, spread 15g butter over the breast and legs of the pheasant and place breast-side down in the casserole. Allow it to brown over a gentle heat, turn over and sprinkle with salt and freshly ground pepper. Cover with a tight-fitting lid and cook in the oven for 40–45 minutes. Check to see that the pheasant is cooked (there should be no trace of pink between the leg and the breast.) Transfer the pheasant to a serving dish and keep warm.

Carefully strain and de-grease the juices in the casserole. Bring to the boil, add the Calvados and ignite with a match. Shake the pan and when the flames have subsided, add the cream or stock and cream. Reduce until the sauce thickens, to a light coating consistency, stirring occasionally; taste for seasoning. The sauce may also thickened by whisking in a little roux.

Fry and toss the apple in the remaining butter over a medium heat until golden. Carve the pheasant and arrange on a hot serving dish or individual plates. Coat with the sauce.

Put the apple in the centre and garnish the dish with watercress or chervil.

POACHED TURKEY WITH MUSHROOMS

Serves 20–25

Another gem, this is a brilliant and delicious party dish. Make it ahead and reheat for stress-free entertaining.

1 x 4.5kg organic, free-range turkey

3.4 litres homemade light chicken stock or water

2 large carrots, sliced

2 large onions, quartered

2 sticks of celery

a bouquet garni made up of 6 parsley stalks,
    2 sprigs of thyme, 1 small bay leaf,
    1 sprig of tarragon

10 peppercorns

900g mushrooms, breakfast flats have best flavour

30–55g salted butter

900ml cream or creamy milk

110g roux (page 76)

sea salt and freshly ground black pepper

watercress, chervil or flat-leaf parsley sprigs,
    to garnish

Put the turkey into a large saucepan. Pour in the chicken stock or water, add the carrots, onions, celery, bouquet garni and peppercorns. Season with salt and freshly ground pepper. Bring to the boil, cover and simmer on the hob or cook in the oven at 180°C/gas mark 4 for 2–2½ hours. When the turkey is cooked, remove from the pot, strain and de-grease the cooking liquid. Discard the vegetables – they will have given their flavour to the cooking juices already. Reduce the liquid by half.

Meanwhile, sauté the sliced mushrooms in the butter in a very hot pan and set aside.

Add the cream or creamy milk to the turkey poaching liquid and reduce again, uncovered, for 5–10 minutes. Add the mushrooms and taste.

Skin the turkey, carve the flesh into 5cm pieces and add to the sauce. Return to the boil and season to taste. (The boiling sauce can be thickened to the required consistency by whisking in roux, rather than reduction if you wish.) Transfer to a hot serving dish and garnish with parsley, chervil or watercress. Serve with a good green salad, pilaff rice or potatoes.

Alternatively, put the turkey in several large serving dishes; if mashed potato is spooned around the edges it's a whole meal in one dish. Reheat later in the oven at 180°C/gas mark 4 for 20–30 minutes.

ROAST DUCK with Bramley apple sauce & red cabbage

Serves 4

This is such a time-honoured combination, the slightly tart Bramley apple sauce cuts the richness of the duck and the braised red cabbage complements the flavour not just of duck but also roast goose and pork with crackling (page 78). Red cabbage is in season in autumn and throughout the winter, however it is now available in summer but tends to be less tender. Some varieties of red cabbage are quite tough and don't seem to soften much, even with prolonged cooking. Our favourite variety, Red Drummond, gives the best results. Serve with venison, duck, goose or pork – the flavour is too strong to accompany fish and delicate meats. The recipe for Braised Red Cabbage serves 8–10 but it keeps brilliantly. Store in the fridge or freeze.

1 x 1.8kg free-range duck

For the stock

neck and giblets from the duck

1 onion, quartered

1 carrot, sliced

bouquet garni made of parsley stalks,
    small celery stalk, sprig of thyme

2–3 peppercorns

salt and freshly ground black pepper

For the sage & onion stuffing

45g salted butter

75g onion, finely chopped

100g soft white breadcrumbs

1 tablespoon freshly chopped sage

sea salt and freshly ground black pepper

For the braised red cabbage

225g red cabbage (Red Drummond if possible)

225g cooking apples, such as Bramley Seedling

½ tablespoon wine vinegar

60ml water

½ level teaspoon salt

1 heaped tablespoon granulated sugar

For the Bramley apple sauce

450g Bramley Seedling cooking apples

1–2 dessertspoons water

approx. 50g sugar depending on tartness
    of the apples

Brining the duck in advance of cooking can enhance the flavour considerably. The day before cooking brine the duck – mix 105g salt with 1.2 litres of water and pop the bird into the brine. Cover and leave overnight.

You'll need some stock to make a flavoursome gravy so use the giblets. To make the stock, put the neck, gizzard, heart and any other trimmings from the duck into a saucepan with the onion, carrot and bouquet garni. Cover with cold water and add the peppercorns but no salt. Bring slowly to the boil and simmer for 2–3 hours. This will make a delicious stock which will be the basis of the gravy.

continued overleaf

Meanwhile, singe the duck if necessary and make the stuffing. Preheat the oven to 180°C/gas mark 4.

To make the stuffing, melt the butter then add the onion and sweat over a gentle heat for 5–10 minutes until soft but not coloured, add the breadcrumbs and sage. Season with salt and freshly ground pepper to taste. Unless you plan to cook the duck immediately leave the stuffing to cool completely.

Season the cavity of the duck with salt and freshly ground pepper and spoon in the cold stuffing. Truss the duck loosely. Roast in the oven for about 1½ hours.

For the braised red cabbage, remove any damaged outer leaves from the cabbage. Examine and clean it if necessary. Cut into quarters, remove the core and slice the cabbage finely across the grain. Put the vinegar, water, salt and sugar into a cast-iron casserole or stainless steel saucepan. Add the cabbage and bring it to the boil.

Meanwhile, peel and core the apples and cut into quarters (no smaller). Lay them on top of the cabbage, cover and continue to cook gently for 30–50 minutes until the cabbage is tender. Do not overcook or the colour and flavour will be ruined. Season to taste and add more sugar if necessary.

To make the Bramley apple sauce, peel, quarter and core the apples, cut the pieces in two and put in a small stainless steel or cast-iron saucepan with the water and sugar. Cover and cook over a low heat. As soon as the apple has broken down, beat into a purée, stir and taste for sweetness.

When the duck is cooked remove to a serving dish and leave to rest while you make the gravy. De-grease the cooking juices (keep the precious duck fat for roast or sauté potatoes). Add the stock to the juices in the roasting pan, bring to the boil, taste and season if necessary. Strain the gravy into a sauceboat and serve with the duck alongside the braised red cabbage and Bramley apple sauce.

CASSEROLE ROAST CHICKEN with leeks & bacon

Serves 4–6

Another delicious casserole roast chicken recipe. Replace the bacon with chorizo or merguez sausage for a more gutsy flavour.

450g leeks, trimmed

225g streaky bacon

1 x 1.5kg organic, free-range chicken

15g salted butter

a splash of sunflower oil

250ml homemade chicken stock or water

250ml light cream

roux (optional – page 76)

salt and freshly ground black pepper

15g freshly chopped flat-leaf parsley, to garnish

Preheat the oven to 180°C/gas mark 4.

Cut the white part of the leeks into rounds and wash them well. Cut the rind from the bacon and cut into 1cm cubes.

Remove the fat from inside the vent end of the chicken and discard. Season with salt and freshly ground pepper. Rub the butter over the breast and legs of the chicken and put it breast-side down into a casserole. Allow it to brown over a gentle heat; this can take 5–6 minutes. As soon as the breast is golden, remove from the casserole and set aside. Add the pieces of bacon to the casserole with a splash of oil. Cook the bacon until the fat runs and the bacon is golden, then add the sliced leeks and toss together in the bacon fat. Season with freshly ground pepper, but no salt as the bacon will probably be salty enough. Then replace the chicken on top of the leeks and bacon. Cover the casserole and roast in the oven for 1¼–1½ hours.

When the chicken is cooked, remove to a serving dish. Lift out the leeks and bacon with a slotted spoon and put into the centre of a hot serving dish.

Skim the juices of all fat, add the chicken stock and cream, and bring to the boil. Thicken by whisking in a little roux. The sauce should not be too thick, just thick enough to lightly coat the back of a spoon. Simmer over a low heat while you carve the chicken.

Carve the chicken into 4–6 helpings, depending on how hungry you all are; everyone should get a portion of white and brown meat. Arrange the leeks and bacon around the chicken. Taste the sauce and add a little more salt and freshly ground pepper if necessary. If the sauce has become too thick, add a little water. Spoon the hot sauce over the chicken, sprinkle with lots of coarsely chopped parsley and serve.

CHICKEN WITH ROSEMARY & TOMATOES

Serves 4–6

I love this chicken dish. Increase the quantity of potatoes and onions to make a more substantial dish, or try using pheasant or guinea fowl for a more gamey flavour.

1 x 1.6kg organic, free-range chicken
30g salted butter
3 onions
3 potatoes
5–6 very ripe tomatoes

sprig of rosemary or 1 teaspoon fresh
   thyme leaves
1 tablespoon extra virgin olive oil
salt and freshly ground black pepper
flat-leaf parsley or marjoram sprigs, to garnish

Preheat the oven to 180°C/gas mark 4.

If possible, remove the wishbone from the neck end of the chicken for ease of carving. Remove the fat from the vent end of the chicken and set aside. Season the cavity with salt and freshly ground pepper. Smear the breast with half the butter, put the chicken breast-side down into a casserole (preferably an oval one that will just fit the chicken) and brown over a gentle heat for 5–6 minutes.

Meanwhile, peel and thickly slice the onions, potatoes and tomatoes. Chop the rosemary finely. Remove the chicken to a plate, add the remaining butter and the extra virgin olive oil to the casserole. Toss the potatoes, onions and tomatoes in the fat and oil. Sprinkle with chopped rosemary, salt and freshly ground pepper. Cover and cook for 5–6 minutes. Put the chicken on top of the vegetables and cover. Cook in the oven for about 1¼ hours.

Carve the chicken and serve with the potatoes, tomatoes and onions. De-grease the juices, bring to the boil and spoon over the chicken and vegetables. Serve sprinkled with sprigs of flat-leaf parsley or marjoram.

Good to know: The organic chicken fat can be rendered down in a low oven (140°C/gas mark 1) and used to roast or sauté potatoes.

CHICKEN PILAFF

Serves 8

A brilliant recipe but you'll need a really flavourful chicken for this – we often use our 'old hens', two-year-old fowl that have come to the end of their laying life and have a deep, rich flavour. The type of bird that the French love to use for coq au vin. Because of their age they need to be poached rather than roasted, otherwise the meat can be tough.

This dish is great for a party. Although a risotto can be made in 20 minutes it entails 20 minutes of pretty constant stirring which makes it feel rather labour intensive. A pilaff on the other hand looks after itself once the initial cooking is underway. The pilaff is versatile – serve it as a staple or add whatever tasty bits you have to hand. Beware of using pilaff as a dustbin, all additions should be carefully seasoned and balanced. It may be prepared ahead of time and reheats well but do not add the liaison until just before serving.

1 x 1.8–2kg organic boiling fowl or free-range, organic chicken

1 large carrot, sliced

1 large onion, sliced

5 peppercorns

a bouquet garni made up of a sprig of thyme, parsley stalks, a tiny bay leaf, a stick of celery

450–600ml water or a mixture of water and white wine or homemade light chicken stock

250–300ml light cream or creamy milk

30g roux (page 76)

sea salt and freshly ground black pepper

watercress sprigs, to serve

For the liaison

1 organic, free-range egg yolk

50ml whipping cream

For the pilaff rice

25g salted butter

2 tablespoons finely chopped onion or shallot

400g long-grain rice (preferably basmati)

975ml homemade chicken stock

2 tablespoons freshly chopped herbs, such as parsley, thyme or chives (optional)

Brine the chicken overnight if time allows. Otherwise, before cooking season the chicken with salt and freshly ground pepper. Put into a heavy casserole with the carrot, onion, peppercorns and bouquet garni. Pour in the water, water and wine or stock (¾ stock to ¼ wine). Cover and bring to the boil and simmer either on the hob or cook in the oven at 180°C/gas mark 4 for 1½–3 hours, depending on the age of the bird. When the bird is cooked, remove from the casserole. The meat should be almost falling off the bones.

Meanwhile, make the pilaff rice. Melt the butter in a casserole, add the onion and sweat for 2–3 minutes. Add the rice and toss for a minute or two, just long enough for the grains to change colour. Season with salt and freshly ground pepper, add the chicken stock, cover and

continued overleaf

bring to the boil. Reduce the heat to a minimum and then simmer the hob or cook in the oven at 160°C/gas mark 3 for about 10 minutes. By then the rice should be just cooked and all the water absorbed. Just before serving stir in the fresh herbs if using.

Strain and de-grease the cooking liquid and return to the casserole. Discard the vegetables: they have already given their flavour to the cooking liquid. Reduce the liquid in a wide, uncovered casserole for 5–10 minutes until the flavour is concentrated. Add the cream or creamy milk, return to the boil and reduce again; thicken to a light coating consistency by whisking in some roux. Add salt to taste.

Skin the chicken and carve the flesh into bite-sized pieces; add to the sauce and heat through and bubble (the dish may be prepared ahead to this point).

Finally, just before serving, whisk the egg yolk and cream together to make a liaison. Add some of the hot sauce to the liaison then carefully stir into the chicken mixture. Season to taste. Stir well but do not allow to boil further or the sauce will curdle. Serve with the pilaff rice and sprigs of watercress.

CHICKEN WITH CREAM & LEMON

Serves 4

You'll love this simple recipe that can be made ahead and gently reheated later. The dish can be embellished with asparagus or seakale in season, or with exotic mushrooms which are available year round. A little chopped marjoram is also wonderful added to the sauce. Finely chopped watercress is also an excellent addition. If all cream seems too rich for your palate, use half cream and half rich chicken stock instead.

4 organic, free-range skinless chicken breasts
25g salted butter
250ml whipping cream
zest and juice of 1 organic, unwaxed lemon

roux (optional - page 76)
sea salt and freshly ground black pepper
finely chopped chives and chive blossoms in
    season, to garnish

Heat a sauté pan just large enough to fit the chicken. Smear the chicken breasts on the skin side with the butter. When the pan is moderately hot place the breasts in the pan, buttered side down. Cook until pale golden brown. Turn and seal on the other side. Season with salt and freshly ground pepper and cover tightly. Cook over a gentle heat for 6–8 minutes depending on size or until the meat is just cooked. Remove the chicken and keep warm.

Add the cream, lemon zest and juice to the pan. Allow to bubble up and simmer until the sauce is gently thickened. Alternatively, add a little roux, just enough to thicken to a light coating consistency. Season to taste. Slide the warm cooked chicken back into the pan and turn in the sauce, then bubble gently for a minute or two.

Serve immediately with a sprinkling of chopped chives or leave to cool and reheat gently at a later stage. Serve with rice, fresh noodles or fettuccine.

meat

GREEK LAMB with onion & butter bean stew

Serves 6

An easy comforting stew that can be adapted and added to – try goat meat if you can source it, it makes a delicious substitute for lamb. I sometimes add a can of tomatoes and their juice, then reduce the stock to 150ml. Add a good pinch of sugar and of course chop the tomatoes. Stir in a heaped tablespoon of annual marjoram or oregano just before serving.

225g butter beans
2 tablespoons extra virgin olive oil
1 x 1.1kg shoulder of lamb, cut into 4cm cubes
680g baby onions, peeled
6 whole garlic cloves, peeled
2 bay leaves

generous sprig of thyme
425–570ml homemade lamb or chicken stock
1 teaspoon salt
freshly ground black pepper
coarsely chopped flat-leaf parsley, to garnish

The day before you want to serve the stew, cover the butter beans with plenty of cold water and leave to soak overnight.

Next day, cover the butter beans with fresh water and cook for 10–15 minutes while you prepare the meat.

Heat the olive oil in a pan, toss the lamb, onions and garlic in the hot pan in batches and transfer to a casserole. Drain the butter beans and add to the casserole with the bay leaves and a large sprig of thyme. Pour in the stock, it should come about halfway up the meat. Add the salt, bring to the boil and simmer for about 1 hour or until all the ingredients are tender. Season to taste, it may need more seasoning. The stew should be nice and juicy but if there is more juice than is necessary remove the lid towards the end of cooking. If the liquid tastes a little weak, strain off the juice and reduce it to the required strength and quantity, in a wide, uncovered pan.

Return the meat and beans to the pan, reheat and season to taste. Sprinkle with coarsely chopped parsley and serve.

LAMB ROAST with rosemary & garlic

Serves 8–10

Rosemary survives year-round even in colder gardens. Spike your leg of lamb with little tufts of this pungent herb and tiny slivers of garlic – delicious hot, warm or at room temperature. A Ballymaloe classic. A little piece of of anchovy wrapped around the rosemary and garlic adds extra flavour.

1 x 2.7–3.2kg leg of lamb
3 sprigs of rosemary, depending on size
3–4 garlic cloves
flaky salt and freshly ground black pepper

For the gravy
600ml homemade lamb stock
roux (optional – page 76)
salt and freshly ground black pepper

Choose a good leg of lamb with a thin layer of fat. Ask the butcher to trim the knuckle and remove the aitch bone for ease of carving later. With the point of a sharp knife or skewer, make deep holes all over the lamb, about 2.5cm apart. It is a good idea not to do this on the underside of the joint, in case somebody insists on eating their lamb unflavoured. Divide the rosemary sprigs into tufts of three or four leaves together.

Peel the garlic cloves and cut them into little spikes about the same size as a matchstick broken into three. Stick a spike of garlic into each hole with a tuft of rosemary. If time allows, cover and chill for an hour or two.

Preheat the oven to 180°C/gas mark 4. Sprinkle the joint with flaky salt and freshly ground pepper and put it into a roasting tin in the oven. Cook for about 1¼ hours for rosy lamb, 1½–1¾ hours if it is to be better done, depending on the size of the joint. If you own a meat thermometer, it will eliminate guesswork altogether, but ensure the thermometer is not touching a bone when you are testing the internal temperature. For rare it should be 60°C, medium 70°C and well done 75°C.

Remove the lamb to a serving dish and leave to rest while you make the gravy.

To make the gravy, spoon the fat off the roasting tin. Pour the stock into the cooking juices remaining in the tin. Boil for a few minutes, stirring and scraping the pan well to dissolve the caramelised meat juices (I find a small whisk is best). Thicken with a very little roux if you like. Season to taste. Strain and serve the gravy separately in a gravy boat. Serve with the lamb roast potatoes or haricot beans.

STEAK WITH BÉARNAISE SAUCE & frites

Serves 6–12,
depending on
how it's served

This is still *the* classic combination. Of all the sauces to serve with steak, béarnaise is my absolute favourite. The consistency should be considerably thicker than that of hollandaise or beurre blanc, both of which ought to be a light coating consistency. Leftover béarnaise sauce solidifies somewhat, we now refer to it as béarnaise butter. Serve a dollop on top of steaks or with roast beef. I find a heavy-ridged, cast-iron grill pan the best for cooking steaks when you don't need to make a sauce in the pan. Rather than serving a steak whole I now prefer to slice it thinly and serve the juicy slices over a bed of rocket or watercress with the frites and a few flakes of sea salt sprinkled on top.

6 x 175g sirloin or fillet steaks

1 garlic clove, peeled

a little extra virgin olive oil

1kg potatoes such as Golden Wonder or Kerr's
   Pink, peeled and cut into 5mm batons

good-quality sunflower or olive oil, for deep-frying

flaky salt and freshly ground black pepper

fresh watercress or rocket leaves (optional),
   to serve

For the béarnaise sauce

4 tablespoons tarragon vinegar (page 74)

4 tablespoons dry white wine

2 teaspoons finely chopped shallots

a pinch of freshly ground black pepper

2 organic, free-range egg yolks

115–175g salted butter

1 tablespoon freshly chopped French tarragon
   leaves, plus extra to garnish

Prepare the steaks about 1 hour before cooking. Score the fat of sirloin steaks at 2.5cm intervals. Cut the garlic clove in half; rub both sides of each steak with the garlic, grind lots of black pepper over the steaks and sprinkle on a few drops of olive oil. Turn the steaks in the oil and set aside at room temperature.

To make the béarnaise sauce, boil the vinegar, wine, shallots and pepper together in a low-sided, heavy-bottomed, stainless steel saucepan until completely reduced and the pan is almost dry but not brown. Add 1 tablespoon of cold water immediately. Remove the pan from the heat and leave to cool for 1–2 minutes.

Whisk in the egg yolks and add the cubes of butter bit by bit over a very low heat, whisking all the time. As soon as one piece melts, add the next piece; the sauce will gradually thicken. If it shows signs of becoming too thick or slightly scrambling, remove from the heat immediately and add a splash of cold water. Do not leave the pan or stop whisking until the sauce is made. Finally add the tarragon and season to taste.

If the sauce is slow to thicken it may be because you are being too cautious and the heat is too low. Increase the heat slightly and continue to whisk until all the butter is added and the sauce

continued overleaf

is a thick coating consistency. It is important to remember, however, that if you are making béarnaise sauce in a saucepan directly over the heat, it should be possible to put your hand on the side of the saucepan at any stage. If the saucepan feels too hot for your hand it is also too hot for the sauce.

Another good tip if you are making béarnaise sauce for the first time is to keep a bowl of cold water close by so that you can plunge the bottom of the saucepan into it if it becomes too hot. Keep the sauce warm in a Pyrex bowl over hot but not simmering water or in a Thermos flask until you want to serve it.

Heat the grill pan, season the steaks with a little flaky salt and put them onto the hot pan. The approximate cooking times for each side of the sirloin steaks are: rare – 2 minutes; medium rare – 3 minutes; medium – 4 minutes and well done – 5 minutes. For fillet steaks: rare – 5 minutes; medium rare – 6 minutes; medium – 7 minutes and well done – 8–9 minutes. I like to start a sirloin steak on the fat side, cook for 4–5 minutes until the fat renders out and becomes deliciously crisp, then cook on each side to your taste.

Transfer the steak onto a plate and leave to rest for a few minutes in a warm place while you cook the frites.

Deep-fry the potatoes in the oil at 160°C until they are almost soft. Then drain and pop them back in for a minute or two at 180–190°C or until crisp and golden. Drain on kitchen paper and sprinkle with a little salt.

Serve on hot plates with the béarnaise sauce over the steak or in a little bowl on the side and sprinkle over a little chopped tarragon. Serve with the frites and fresh watercress. Alternatively, thinly slice the steak and serve on a bed of watercress or rocket leaves, drizzle with béarnaise sauce and serve as soon as possible.

TIP

⁓ Tarragon vinegar is essential for béarnaise sauce. It's not easy to find but it's super easy to make, just push 3–4 sprigs of fresh tarragon into a bottle of good-quality wine vinegar and leave to infuse for 6–7 days before using. Some of the pickled tarragon may also be added to the béarnaise sauce. If you do not have tarragon vinegar to hand, use a wine vinegar and add some extra chopped tarragon to the béarnaise sauce.

BALLYMALOE BACON CHOP

Serves 5–6

At Ballymaloe House we serve Bacon Chop with Irish Whiskey Sauce, but it is also delicious served just with simple fried bananas – it sounds passé but believe me it's *so* good. Seek out home-cured bacon from heirloom pigs, if you can. We cure our own bacon from our free-range saddleback pigs, or we ask our local butcher Frank Murphy to cure it for us. We particularly love to serve these bacon chops with piperonata and champ.

1 x 1kg loin of bacon (boneless and without the streaky end), freshly cured

110g seasoned plain flour

1 organic egg, beaten with a little milk

fresh, white breadcrumbs or panko crumbs

25g clarified butter (page 185) or 15g salted butter and 1–2 tablespoons olive oil, for frying

For the fried banana

15g salted butter

2 bananas

For the Irish whiskey sauce

225g granulated sugar

75ml cold water

60ml hot water

3–4 tablespoons Irish whiskey

Place the piece of bacon in a saucepan and cover with cold water. Bring to the boil. If the bacon is excessively salty, there will be a white froth on top of the water so throw out the water and start again. After the blanching process bring the water to the boil and continue to boil for 45 minutes–1 hour or until fully cooked. Remove the rind but not the fat unless it is too much. Slice into chops 2cm thick.

Dip each chop in seasoned flour, then in the beaten egg and finally coat with the breadcrumbs. Heat clarified butter and oil in a heavy frying pan, cook the chops gently until they are cooked through and golden on both sides.

To make the fried bananas, melt the butter in a frying pan. Peel the bananas then split in half lengthways or cut in thick slices diagonally. Fry gently in the melted butter until soft and slightly golden.

To make the Irish whiskey sauce, put the sugar into a saucepan with the cold water and stir over a gentle heat until the sugar dissolves and the syrup comes to the boil. Remove the spoon and do not stir. Continue to boil until it turns a nice chestnut-brown colour. Remove from the heat and immediately add the hot water. Allow to dissolve again and then add the Irish whiskey. Serve hot or cold alongside the bacon chop and fried bananas.

BALLYMALOE IRISH STEW

Serves 4–6

Another classic one-pot dish. The recipe varies from region to region – in Cork, carrots are a quintessential addition, not so in parts of Ulster. Pearl barley is another favourite option, originally added to bulk up the stew. You'll need to add extra stock (300–600ml) if you include pearl barley, it guzzles up liquid but becomes deliciously plump and flavourful.

1.35kg lamb chops (gigot or rack chops)
   not less than 2.5cm thick
8 medium or 12 baby onions
12 baby carrots, peeled and cut into large chunks
1–2 tablespoons pearl barley (optional)
850ml–1 litre homemade lamb stock or water
8–12 large potatoes, or more if you like, peeled
1 sprig of thyme

1 tablespoon roux (see below – optional)
1 tablespoon freshly chopped parsley
1 tablespoon freshly chopped chives
salt and freshly ground black pepper
For the roux
110g salted butter
110g plain flour or 50g cornflour and 50g rice flour,
   for a gluten-free roux

Preheat the oven to 180°C/gas mark 4.

Cut the chops in half and trim off some of the excess fat. Set aside. Render the lamb fat over a gentle heat in a heavy frying pan (discard the rendered down pieces).

Toss the meat in the hot fat in the pan until it is slightly brown. Transfer the meat into a casserole, then quickly toss the onions and carrots in the fat, and the pearl barley, if using. Build the meat, carrots and onions (and pearl barley) up in layers in the casserole, carefully season *each layer* with freshly ground pepper and salt. De-grease the pan with the lamb stock, bring to the boil and pour into the casserole. Lay the potatoes on top of the casserole (they will steam while the stew cooks). Season the potatoes, add a sprig of thyme, bring to the boil on the hob, cover with a paper lid and the casserole lid. Transfer to the oven or leave to simmer on the hob for 1½ hours until the stew is cooked. The cooking time will depend on whether the stew is being made with lamb or hogget.

To make the roux, melt the butter and cook the flour (or cornflour and rice flour) in it for 2 minutes over a low heat, stirring occasionally. Roux can be stored in a cool place and used as required or it can be made up on the spot. It will keep for at least 2 weeks in the fridge.

When the stew is cooked, pour off the cooking liquid, de-grease and reheat the juices in another saucepan. Thicken slightly by whisking in a little roux. Check the seasoning, then add half the freshly chopped parsley and chives. Pour over the meat and vegetables. Bring the stew back up to boiling point and serve from the pot or in a large pottery dish sprinkled with the remaining chopped herbs. Serve in deep plates with lots of good Irish butter.

CRACKLING ROAST PORK

with garlic & thyme leaves & Bramley apple sauce

Serves 10–12

Streaky pork is less expensive than loin and makes the sweetest and juiciest roast pork. Make sure to buy it with the skin on otherwise you'll miss out on the crackling. The trick with apple sauce is to cook it covered over a low heat with very little water. Apple sauce freezes perfectly, so make more than you need and freeze in tiny, plastic cartons. It is also a good way to use up windfalls.

1 x 2.3kg joint of organic streaky pork,
    preferably heirloom
Mix or blend of the following: 3 finely chopped
    garlic cloves, 4 tablespoons freshly chopped
    parsley, 1 tablespoon olive oil (add more if
    needed to make a thick paste), 2 tablespoons
    fresh thyme leaves, 1 teaspoon flaky sea salt,
    1 teaspoon freshly ground black pepper

For the gravy
1 litre homemade chicken or pork stock
roux (optional – page 76)
For the Bramley apple sauce
450g cooking apples, such as Bramley Seedling
    or Grenadier
1–2 dessertspoons water
55g granulated sugar, depending on how tart the
    apples are

Score the pork skin at 5mm intervals, a Stanley knife works brilliantly, otherwise you may want to ask your butcher to do this because the skin of free-range pork can be quite tough. (Scoring will make it easier to carve later.) Rub the herb paste well into the cuts, it should not be sitting on top.

Preheat the oven to 180°C/gas mark 4. Roast the pork on a rack over a roasting tin, allowing 28–30 minutes per 450g. Just before the end of cooking transfer the joint to another roasting tin and increase the temperature to 230°C/gas mark 8 to crisp the crackling.

Peel, quarter and core the apples. Cut the pieces into two and put in a stainless steel or cast-iron saucepan with the water and sugar. Cover and cook over a low heat. As soon as the apples have broken down, beat into a purée, stir and taste for sweetness. Serve warm.

To make the gravy, de-grease the roasting tin and add the stock to deglaze. Bring to the boil, season, and whisk to dissolve any caramelised pork juices. Thicken with a little roux if desired. Add lots of freshly chopped herbs, such as parsley, thyme and maybe a tiny scrap of sage to the gravy. Serve with roast potatoes, preferably cooked in pork lard, and the Bramley apple sauce.

DINGLE PIE

Mutton and lamb pies were, and still are, traditional in many parts of Co Kerry, including Dingle and Listowel. Cumin was not part of the original recipe but was an addition by Myrtle Allen, which Ballymaloe House guests loved. The original pastry was made with lamb suet but Myrtle substituted butter with delicious results. This pie freezes perfectly for 2–3 months but use sooner rather than later. The quantity of cumin seeds will depend on how fresh the spice is.

450g boneless lamb or mutton (from the shoulder
    or leg; keep bones for stock)
250g onions
250g carrots
1–2 good teaspoons cumin seeds
2 tablespoons plain flour
300ml homemade lamb or mutton stock
    (see below)
sea salt and freshly ground black pepper

For the lamb or mutton stock
lamb bones from the meat
1 carrot
1 onion
outside stalk of celery
a bouquet garni made up of a sprig of thyme,
    parsley stalks
1 small bay leaf

For the pastry
350g plain white flour
a pinch of salt
1 organic egg, beaten
175g butter
110ml water

To make the stock, put the lamb bones, carrot, onion, celery and bouquet garni into a saucepan. Cover with cold water and simmer for 3–4 hours.

Trim all the surplus fat from the meat, dice the meat into small, neat pieces about the size of a small sugar lump. Render down the scraps of fat in a hot, wide saucepan until the fat runs. Discard the pieces. Cut the onions and carrots into slightly smaller dice and toss them in the fat, leaving them to cook for 3–4 minutes. Remove the vegetables and toss the meat in the remaining fat over a high heat until the colour changes.

Dry roast the cumin seeds in a hot frying pan for a few minutes and crush lightly. Stir the flour and cumin seeds into the meat. Cook gently for 2 minutes and blend the stock in gradually. Bring to the boil, stirring occasionally. Return the vegetables to the pan, season with salt and freshly ground pepper and leave to simmer, covered. If using young lamb, 30 minutes will be sufficient; an older animal may take up to 1 hour.

continued overleaf

Meanwhile, make the pastry. Sift the flour and salt into a mixing bowl and make a well in the centre. Dice the butter, put it into a saucepan with the measured water and bring to the boil. Pour the liquid into the flour all at once and mix together quickly; beat until smooth. At first the pastry will be too soft to handle but as soon as it cools it may be rolled out 2.5–5mm thick, to fit two 15cm tins, 4cm high. The pastry may be made into individual pies or one large pie (use a 17.5cm tart tin). Keep back one-third of the pastry for lids.

Preheat the oven to 220°C/gas mark 7.

Fill the pastry-lined tins with the meat mixture, which should be just cooked and cooled a little. Brush the edges of the pastry with a little water and put on the pastry lids, pressing them tightly together. Roll out the trimmings to make pastry leaves or twirls to decorate the top of the pies; make a hole in the centre. Eggwash the lid and then eggwash the decoration also.

Bake the pies for about 40 minutes. Serve with a salad of seasonal leaves.

VARIATION
— Puff pastry can be substituted for the hot water crust pastry.

BEEF WITH STOUT

Serves 6–8

Use your favourite stout for this recipe. In Cork we use Beamish or Murphy, but even Cork people have divided allegiances! Ireland now has a whole new generation of artisan and craft brewers – we've got quite the choice. Experiment with your local brew: Eight Degrees, Franciscan Well, Dungarvan – each gives the stew its own characteristic flavour.

900g stewing beef, preferably marbled with a little fat, such as chuck or shin

seasoned plain flour

3 tablespoons olive oil

2 onions, thinly sliced

125ml Beamish, Murphy or Guinness

425ml beef stock

1 tablespoon granulated sugar

1 teaspoon English mustard powder

1 tablespoon concentrated tomato purée (page 18)

1 strip of dried orange peel

a bouquet garni made up of 1 bay leaf, 1 sprig of fresh thyme, 4 parsley stalks

225g flat mushrooms

15g salted butter

salt and freshly ground black pepper

coarsely chopped flat-leaf parsley, to garnish

Preheat the oven to 150°C/gas mark 2.

Cut the meat into 4cm cubes and toss in the seasoned flour. Heat some of the olive oil in a hot pan and fry the meat in batches until it is brown on all sides. Transfer the meat to a casserole and add a little more oil to the pan. Fry the onions until nicely browned; deglaze with the stout. Transfer to the casserole, add the stock, sugar, mustard, tomato purée, orange peel and bouquet garni. Season with salt and freshly ground pepper. Bring to the boil, cover and transfer to the oven to cook for 2–2½ hours or until the meat is tender.

Meanwhile, wash and slice the mushrooms. Sauté in the butter in a hot pan. Season with salt and freshly ground pepper. Set aside. When the stew is cooked, add the mushrooms and simmer for 2–3 minutes then season to taste. Serve sprinkled with lots of chopped parsley.

This stew reheats well and improves with keeping for a day or two in the fridge. You may need to add more sugar to the recipe if you find it a little bitter from the stout.

ITALIAN BEEF STEW

A super recipe for a beef stew, unusually it doesn't have pickled bacon or pickled pork, but you could add a few chunks. It's still a firm favourite after all these years, although we now serve it with some gremolata sprinkled over the top. Italian beef stew, like many other stews, is even better when served next day, it reheats deliciously over a gentle heat the hob or in a low oven and freezes brilliantly. Leftover stew, with or without any chunks of meat, makes a delicious sauce for pasta, just add a generous grating of Parmesan and some freshly chopped parsley

1.35kg well-hung stewing beef or lean flank
olive oil, for frying
2 large carrots, cut into 1cm slices
285g sliced onions
1 heaped tablespoon plain flour
150ml red wine
150ml brown beef stock
250ml homemade tomato purée (see left)
140g sliced mushrooms (flats have more flavour)
1 tablespoon freshly chopped flat-leaf parsley
salt and freshly ground black pepper

For the tomato purée
900g very ripe tomatoes
1 small onion, chopped
1 teaspoon granulated sugar
a good pinch of salt and a few twists of
    black pepper
For the gremolata
4 tablespoons freshly chopped flat-leaf parsley
1 generous teaspoon grated or finely chopped
    lemon zest
2 garlic cloves, finely chopped

To make the tomato purée, cut the ripe tomatoes into quarters, put into a stainless steel saucepan with the onion, sugar, salt and freshly ground pepper. Cook over a gentle heat until the tomatoes are soft (no water needed). Put through the fine blade of a mouli legumes or a nylon sieve. Leave to get cold then chill or freeze.

Preheat the oven to 160°C/gas mark 3.

Trim the meat of any excess fat, then cut into 4cm cubes. Heat 1 tablespoon of olive oil in a casserole; sweat the sliced carrots and onions over a gentle heat with the lid on for 10 minutes. Heat a little more olive oil in a frying pan until almost smoking. Sear the pieces of meat on all sides, reduce the heat, stir in the flour and cook for 1 minute. Mix the wine, stock and tomato purée together and add gradually to the casserole. Season with salt and freshly ground pepper. Cover and cook gently for 2–3 hours in the oven, depending on the cut of meat.

Meanwhile, sauté the mushrooms in a hot pan in a little olive oil, add to the casserole with the chopped parsley about 30 minutes before the end of cooking.

To make the gremolata, mix all the ingredients together in a small bowl. Serve the stew with polenta, mashed potatoes or noodles and a good green salad.

BOEUF BOURGUIGNON

Serves 6–8

A French classic. In Irleand, stew is generally regarded as something you feed to the family but not your honoured guests. Not so in France, where this recipe for the most famous of all beef stews, Boeuf Bourguignon, might be served for a special Sunday lunch or dinner with friends. After all it is not cheap to make: you need best-quality well-hung stewing beef and the best part of a bottle of red wine. As the name suggests it used to be made with Burgundy, but with current Burgundy prices I think I might settle for a good Beaujolais or a full-bodied Côtes du Rhône.

225g fat streaky bacon

1–2 tablespoons extra virgin olive oil

1.35kg well-hung stewing beef cut into 5cm cubes

1 large carrot, sliced

175g onion, sliced

2 tablespoons brandy (optional)

425ml full-bodied red wine, such as Burgundy,
    Côtes du Rhône or even a Beaujolais

300–450ml brown beef stock

1 tablespoon tomato paste

5cm piece of dried orange peel

1 sprig of thyme

1 bay leaf

3 garlic cloves, peeled

18–24 small onions, depending on size

450g small flat mushrooms, cut into quarters

roux (optional – page 76)

sea salt and freshly ground black pepper

Remove the rind from the bacon (roll up, tie and save). Cut the bacon into 1cm cubes. Blanch and refresh if salty then dry well on kitchen paper. Heat the olive oil in a frying pan, sauté the bacon until crisp and golden and transfer to a casserole.

Increase the heat so that the oil and bacon fat are almost smoking. Dry off the meat. Sauté it, a few pieces at a time, until nicely browned on all sides, then add to the casserole with the bacon. Toss the sliced carrot and onion in the remaining fat and add these too.

If there is any fat left in the pan at this stage pour it off, add the brandy, if using, and flame it then deglaze the pan with wine, scraping the little bits of sediment on the pan until they dissolve. Bring to the boil and pour over the beef, this all adds to the flavour.

The casserole may be prepared ahead to this point. Leave it to get cold, cover and chill overnight, or at least for a few hours. The wine will have a tenderising effect on the meat, and the other ingredients will add extra flavour as the meat marinades.

Later or the following day, add enough stock to almost cover the meat, add in the tomato paste, dried orange peel, thyme, bay leaf and the whole garlic cloves. Season with salt and freshly ground pepper. Bring to the boil, cover and simmer very gently either on top of the stove or in a low oven at 160°C/gas mark 3 for 1½–2½ hours, depending on the cut of meat used. The meat should not fall apart but it should be tender enough to eat without too much chewing.

Meanwhile, cook the small onions. Peel the onions – this task is made easier if you drop them in boiling water for 1 minute, run them under the cold tap, 'top and tail' them and then slip off the skins. Simmer gently in a small covered casserole with about 1cm of water or beef stock – they will take 30–35 minutes depending on size. A knife should pierce them easily.

Toss the quartered mushrooms a few at a time in a little olive oil in a hot pan, and season with salt and freshly ground pepper.

When the meat is tender, pour the contents of the casserole into a strainer or colander placed over a saucepan. Discard the herbs, carrot, onion and orange peel. Return the meat to the casserole with the onions and mushrooms. Skim the fat from the liquid. There should be about 600ml sauce. Taste, return to the boil and simmer. If the sauce is too thin or too weak, reduce for a few minutes, otherwise thicken slightly by whisking in a little roux. Pour over the meat, mushrooms and onions, return to the boil, simmer for a few minutes until heated through and season to taste. Sprinkle with lots of chopped parsley and serve with a rich mashed potato.

Boeuf Bourguignon may be made a few days ahead and the flavour even improves with keeping for a day or two.

TRADITIONAL IRISH BACON
with cabbage & parsley sauce

Serves 12–15

Ireland's national dish of bacon and cabbage can be a sorry disappointment nowadays, partly because it is so difficult to get good-quality bacon with a decent bit of fat on it. Traditionally, the cabbage was always cooked in the bacon water. People could only hang one pot over the fire at a time, so when the bacon was almost cooked, they added the cabbage for the last half hour or 45 minutes of cooking. The bacon water gives a salty, unforgettable flavour, which many people, including me, still hanker for. You will need to order the loin well in advance, especially with rind on. We love the home-cured bacon from Woodside Farm near Midleton.

2.25kg loin, collar or streaky bacon, either smoked or unsmoked with the rind on and a nice covering of fat
1 Savoy or 2 spring hispi cabbages, cut into thin shreds
50g salted butter
freshly ground black pepper

For the parsley sauce
600ml full-cream milk
a few parsley stalks
sprig of thyme
a few slices of carrot (optional)
a few slices of onion (optional)
50g roux (page 76)
50g freshly chopped curly parsley
salt and freshly ground black pepper

Cover the bacon in cold water in a large pan and bring slowly to the boil. If the bacon is very salty there will be a white froth on top of the water, in which case discard the water and start again. Cover with hot water and the lid of the pan and simmer until almost cooked, allowing 25 minutes for every 450g.

About 20 minutes before the end of cooking the bacon, add the shredded cabbage to the water in which the bacon is boiling. Stir, cover and continue to boil gently until both the cabbage and bacon are cooked – about 1¾ hours in total.

To make the parsley sauce, put the cold milk into a saucepan and add the herbs and vegetables (if using). Bring the mixture to simmering point, season and simmer for 4–5 minutes. Strain the milk, bring it back to the boil and whisk in the roux until the sauce is a light coating consistency. Season again with salt and freshly ground pepper. Add the chopped parsley and simmer on a very low heat for 4–5 minutes. Season to taste.

Lift the bacon onto a plate and remove the rind if you like. When the bacon is fully cooked it will peel off easily. Strain the cabbage and discard the water (or, if it's not too salty, save it for a tomato soup). Add a generous lump of butter to the cabbage. Season with lots of ground pepper. Serve the bacon with the cabbage, parsley sauce and floury potatoes.

SPICED LAMB with aubergines

Serves 6

A gorgeous, flavourful stew. It's worth doubling or even tripling the recipe as it keeps and improves in the fridge for several days and freezes perfectly.

1 x 1kg shoulder of lamb
1 heaped teaspoon cumin seeds
3 aubergines
2 tablespoons extra virgin olive oil
200g onions, sliced
1 large garlic clove, sliced

3 teaspoons freshly chopped mint
3 teaspoons freshly chopped marjoram
400g very ripe tomatoes or 1 x 400g can
   chopped tomatoes
sea salt and freshly ground black pepper
fresh coriander leaves, to garnish

Preheat the oven to 180°C/gas mark 4.

Cut the meat into 2.5cm cubes. Dry roast the cumin in a frying pan for a few minutes, crush using a pestle and mortar and sprinkle over the meat. Cut the aubergines into somewhat larger cubes. Sprinkle the aubergine cubes with salt and pop in a colander to drain with a plate on top to weigh them down.

Heat the olive oil in a pan and sweat the sliced onion and garlic. Add the meat and allow it to colour, sprinkle with mint and marjoram and season with salt and freshly ground pepper. Transfer the meat and onions to a casserole. Cover and put in the oven.

Rinse the aubergines and drain, then dry them with kitchen paper. Toss them in the olive oil in the pan, season with salt and freshly ground pepper and allow to colour. Add to the meat, stir and cover.

Meanwhile, skin the tomatoes and put them into the casserole with the meat mixture. Season with flaky sea salt and freshly ground black pepper. Re-cover and cook over a gentle heat or in the oven for about 30 minutes or until the meat is meltingly tender. Season to taste.

De-grease the cooking liquid if necessary. Garnish with lots of fresh coriander leaves and serve with pilaff rice or homemade fettuccine.

FILLET OF BEEF with mushrooms & thyme

Serves 6

Always a treat, this is super rich and delicious – one can alter the proportion of stock to cream if you'd prefer a less unctuous sauce, but the original is wonderful.

1kg well-hung dry-aged fillet steak
   (allow 165g fillet steak per person)
15g butter
1 dessertspoon extra virgin olive oil
salt, freshly ground black pepper and sugar
watercress, chervil or flat-leaf parsley,
   to garnish

For the sauce
30g salted butter
3 tablespoons shallots or spring onions,
   finely chopped
225g sliced button mushrooms
150ml red wine
150ml brown beef stock
290ml single cream
roux (optional – page 76)
1 teaspoon fresh thyme leaves
a few drops of lemon juice

To make the sauce, melt the butter in a frying pan and sweat the shallots over a gentle heat until soft but not coloured; remove from the pan. Increase the heat and sauté the mushrooms a few at a time, season each batch and add to the shallots as soon as they are cooked. Add the wine and stock to the pan and boil rapidly until the liquid has reduced to about 75ml. Add the cream and allow to simmer for a few minutes to thicken (whisk in a tiny bit of roux if you like). Add the sautéed mushroom and onion mixture and the thyme leaves. Simmer for 1–2 minutes; don't allow the sauce to thicken too much or it will be heavy and cloying. Correct the seasoning if necessary. If the sauce tastes a little too rich, add some water and a squeeze of lemon juice. This sauce can be cooked several hours in advance and reheated later.

To prepare the beef, trim the beef of any fat or membrane, cut into 55g pieces. Melt the butter and olive oil in a hot pan and when the foam subsides sauté the beef. Remember not to overcrowd the pan; the pieces of beef will only take 1–3 minutes on each side, depending on how you like it cooked. As soon as the beef is cooked, place the pieces on an upturned plate resting on a larger plate to catch any juices.

To serve, reheat the sauce, serve 3 pieces of steak per person on individual plates or on a large serving plate and coat with the hot mushroom sauce. Garnish with watercress, chervil or flat-leaf parsley.

fish & seafood

MACKEREL WITH MUSHROOMS & HERBS

Serves 4

My father-in-law, Ivan Allen, had a mushroom farm in Shanagarry for many years. This was his favourite way to eat the beautiful mackerel fresh from the little day-boats in Ballycotton. This mushroom, garlic and herb mixture is also delicious served with sautéd chicken livers on toast as a starter.

4 very fresh mackerel
seasoned plain flour
15g clarified butter (page 185)
110g fresh, flat mushrooms, sliced
1–2 garlic cloves, crushed

4 teaspoons finely chopped fresh herbs, such as thyme, parsley, chives, fennel and lemon balm, plus extra to garnish
salt and freshly ground black pepper

Fillet the mackerel, then wash, dry well and dip in the seasoned flour. Melt the butter in a pan large enough to take the fish in a single layer and sauté the fish for 4–5 minutes on each side, depending on the size, until golden on both sides.

Remove the fish to a hot serving dish or four individual plates. Add the mushrooms and garlic to the pan with a little more butter if necessary. Cook over a high heat for 2–3 minutes, add the chopped fresh herbs and season with a little salt and freshly ground pepper if necessary. Serve this mixture as a garnish down the centre of the fish and sprinkle with chopped herbs.

BALLYCOTTON FISH PIE

Serves 6–8

How fortunate are we to live close to the little fishing village of Ballycotton in East Cork? Everyone loves fish pie and the combination I use depends on the fish catch. Omit mussels and shrimps if they are not available. This dish may be served in individual dishes: scallop shells are particularly attractive, are completely ovenproof and may be used over and over again.

1.1kg cod, hake, haddock or grey sea mullet fillets
    or a mixture
15g salted butter
600ml milk
110g cooked mussels, out of shells
110g cooked and peeled shrimp
55g roux (page 76)
¼ teaspoon mustard, preferably Dijon

140–170g grated Irish Cheddar cheese or
    85g grated Parmesan cheese
2 tablespoons freshly chopped parsley
800g fluffy mashed potato or champ (optional)
salt and freshly ground black pepper
For the buttered crumbs
30g salted butter
55g soft white breadcrumbs

Preheat the oven to 180°C/gas mark 4.

Skin the fish and cut into portions: 170g for a main course, 85g for a starter. Season with salt and freshly ground pepper. Lay the pieces of fish in a lightly buttered sauté pan and cover with the cold milk. Bring to the boil, simmer for 4–5 minutes or until the fish has changed colour. Remove the fish to a serving dish or dishes with a slotted spoon. Scatter the mussels and shrimp over the top.

Bring the milk back to the boil and thicken with roux to a light coating consistency. Add the mustard, two-thirds of the grated cheese and the parsley. Keep the remaining cheese for sprinkling over the top. Season well with salt and freshly ground pepper.

Next make the buttered crumbs. Melt the butter in a pan and stir in the breadcrumbs. Remove from the heat immediately and leave to cool.

Coat the fish with the sauce. Pipe fluffy mashed potato or champ in swirls on top for a more substantial dish, if you wish. Mix the remaining grated cheese with the buttered crumbs and sprinkle over the top.

Cook the oven for 15–20 minutes or until heated through and the top is golden brown and crispy. If necessary, place under the grill for a minute or two before you serve, to brown the edge of the potato.

BAKED SUMMER PLAICE with herb butter

Serves 4

A Ballymaloe classic, the simple cooking technique can be used not only for baking plaice and sole but for all very fresh flat fish, such as brill, turbot, dabs, flounder and lemon sole. Because it's cooked whole on the bone, it retains maximum flavour. Peel the skin off the top when cooked and coat with a simple herb butter, hollandaise or beurre blanc sauce. We sometimes add a few peeled shrimp, mussels, cockles or periwinkles to the butter or sauce for an even more exquisite dish.

4 very fresh summer plaice or Dover sole,
   on the bone
salt and freshly ground black pepper

For the herb butter
50–110g salted butter
4 teaspoons mixed finely chopped fresh flat-leaf
   parsley, chives, fennel and thyme leaves

Preheat the oven to 190°C/gas mark 5.

Turn the fish on its side and remove the head. Wash the fish and clean the slit very thoroughly. With a sharp knife, cut through the dark skin right round the fish, just where the 'fringe' meets the flesh. Be careful to cut neatly and to cross the side cuts at the tail or it will be difficult to remove the skin later on.

Sprinkle the fish with salt and freshly ground pepper and lay them in a generous 5mm of water in a shallow baking tin. Bake for 20–30 minutes according to the size of the fish. The water should have almost evaporated as the fish is cooked. Check to see whether the fish is cooked by lifting the flesh from the bone at the head and it should lift off the bone easily and be quite white with no trace of pink.

Just before serving melt the butter and stir in the freshly chopped herbs. To serve, catch the skin down near the tail of the fish and pull it off gently (the skin will tear badly if not properly cut). Lift the fish onto hot plates and spoon the herb butter evenly over the surface of the fish. Serve immediately.

MONKFISH with cucumber & dill hollandaise

Serves 4 or
8 as a starter

Even though its appearance is ugly, monkfish is one of the most sought after fish, firm and succulent with no tiny bones to worry about. What's not to love about monkfish with hollandaise?

675g monkfish tail cut into 1cm collops

1 tablespoon salt

sprigs of dill and dill flowers, to garnish

For the cucumber & dill hollandaise

2 organic, free-range egg yolks

1 dessertspoon cold water

117g salted butter, diced

approx. 1 teaspoon freshly squeezed lemon juice

⅓ cucumber, peeled and cut into tiny dice

1 tablespoon fresh dill, chopped

dill flowers, if in season

First make the hollandaise sauce. Put the egg yolks in a heavy, stainless steel saucepan over a very low heat or in a bowl over hot water. Add the measured water and whisk thoroughly. Add 110g of butter bit by bit, whisking all the time. As soon as one piece melts, add the next piece. The mixture will gradually thicken, but if it shows signs of becoming too thick or slightly scrambling, remove from the heat immediately and add a little cold water if necessary. Do not leave the pan or stop whisking until the sauce is made. Finally add the lemon juice to taste. If the sauce is slow to thicken it may be because you are too cautious and the heat is too low. Increase the heat slightly and continue to whisk until the sauce thickens to a light coating consistency. Pour into a bowl and keep warm.

Melt the remaining butter in a saucepan and toss the tiny dice of cucumber in it for 1–2 minutes. Add to the hollandaise sauce with the freshly chopped dill.

Just before serving, bring 2.3 litres of water to the boil and add 1 tablespoon of salt. Add the monkfish collops, bring back to the boil and simmer for 4–5 minutes or until the pieces are no longer opaque, but completely white and tender. Drain the monkfish thoroughly.

To serve, arrange overlapping pieces of monkfish on individual plates. Whisk in a little hot water if the hollandaise sauce is too thick, it should be a light coating consistency. Spoon carefully over the fish. Garnish with some feathery dill and dill flowers in season. Serve immediately.

COD, HAKE OR HADDOCK
with leeks & buttered crumbs

Serves 6 or 12 as
a starter

The gentle flavour of buttered leeks is particularly good with fish, but the basic recipe with mornay sauce and crunchy crumbs always gets a brilliant reaction. Sautéed mushrooms, tomato fondue or piperonata also complement the flavour of the fish instead of leeks.

1.1kg hake, cod, ling, haddock, grey sea mullet
   or pollock
15g salted butter
salt and freshly ground black pepper
For the mornay sauce
600ml whole milk
a few slices of carrot and onion
3–4 peppercorns
a sprig of thyme and parsley
50g roux (page 76)
¼ teaspoon Dijon mustard

150–175g grated Cheddar cheese or
   75g grated Parmesan cheese
1–2 tablespoons chopped parsley (optional)
For the buttered leeks
25g salted butter
450g leeks, halved and sliced into 5mm rounds
salt and freshly ground black pepper
For the buttered crumbs
25g butter
50g soft white breadcrumbs

First make the mornay sauce. Put the milk into a saucepan with the carrot, onion, peppercorns and herbs. Bring to the boil, simmer for 4–5 minutes, remove from the heat and leave to infuse for 10 minutes. Strain out the vegetables, bring the milk back to the boil and thicken with roux to a coating consistency. Remove from the heat, leave to cool for 1 minute then add the mustard and two-thirds of the grated cheese, keeping the remaining cheese for sprinkling over the top. Season to taste. Add the parsley if using.

Make the buttered leeks. Melt the butter in a heavy casserole; when it foams, add the leeks and toss gently to coat with butter. Season with salt and freshly ground pepper. Cover with a paper lid and a close-fitting lid. Reduce the heat and cook very gently for 8–10 minutes or until semi-soft and moist.

Next make the buttered crumbs. Melt the butter in a pan and stir in the breadcrumbs. Remove from the heat immediately and leave to cool.

Preheat the oven to 180°C/gas mark 4. Skin the fish and cut into portions: 175g for a main course, 75g for a starter. Season with salt and freshly ground pepper. Lightly butter an ovenproof dish, cover the base of the dish with a layer of buttered leeks, coat with some mornay sauce, lay the fish on top and coat with more sauce. Mix the remaining grated cheese with the buttered crumbs and sprinkle over the top. Cook for 25–30 minutes or until the fish is cooked through and the top is golden brown and crispy.

MOULES PROVENÇALE

Serves 6–8

Mussels, although available year-round in Ireland are plumpest and best in the colder months of the year. They are terrifically good value in comparison to other shellfish, very versatile and a perennial favourite; don't skimp on the garlic in this recipe or they will taste rather dull and 'bready'. You can also use this recipe with cockles or palourdes, a type of clam which grows off the West Cork coast, around Kenmare Bay.

48 mussels, preferably wild, approx. 1.5–1.8kg

For the Provençale butter

2 large garlic cloves

2 tablespoons finely chopped parsley

1 tablespoon extra virgin olive oil

75g salted butter, softened

fresh white breadcrumbs

Check that all the mussels are closed. If any are open, tap the mussel on the work top, if they do not close within a few seconds, discard. (The rule with shellfish is always, 'If in doubt, throw it out'.) Scrape off any barnacles from the mussel shells. Wash the mussels well in several changes of cold water. Then spread them in a single layer in a pan, cover with a folded tea towel or a lid and cook over a gentle heat until the shells open. This usually takes 2–3 minutes, the mussels are cooked just as soon as the shells pop open. Remove them from the pan immediately or they will shrink and toughen.

Remove the beard (the little tuft of coarse 'hair' which attached the mussel to the rock or rope it grew on). Discard one shell. Loosen the mussel from the other shell, but leave it in the shell. Leave to get quite cold.

Meanwhile, make the Provençale butter. Peel and crush the garlic and pound it in a mortar with the finely chopped parsley and extra virgin olive oil. Gradually beat in the butter (this may be done either in a bowl or a food processor). Spread the soft garlic butter evenly over the mussels in the shells and dip each one into the soft, white breadcrumbs. They may be prepared ahead to this point and frozen in a covered box lined with clingfilm or parchment paper.

Brown under the grill and serve with crusty white bread to mop up the delicious garlicky juices.

VARIATION

Mussels with Wild Garlic or Watercress Butter Substitute wild garlic or watercress leaves for parsley in the above recipe.

THREE-MINUTE FISH

Serves 4

This is the fastest fish recipe I know and certainly one of the most delicious. It can be fun to mix pink- and white-fleshed fish on the same plate, e.g. salmon and sea bass.

We also love crudo – just lay slices of super fresh fish on a chilled plate. Drizzle freshly squeezed lemon and some extra virgin olive oil over the top and maybe a little sprinkle of fresh sprigs of chervil.

450g fillet of very fresh fish, such as wild Irish salmon, cod, turbot, large sole, sea bass or grey sea mullet
extra virgin olive oil or melted butter

finely chopped fresh herbs such as parsley, thyme, chives, chervil
salt and freshly ground black pepper

Season the fillet of fish with salt and freshly ground pepper about 30 minutes before cutting; chill in the fridge to stiffen it.

Preheat the oven to 230°C/gas mark 8.

While the oven is heating, brush four ovenproof plates with a little extra virgin olive oil or melted butter. Put the fillet of fish on a chopping board skin-side down; cut the flesh into scant 5mm thin slices down onto the skin. Arrange the slices on the base of the ovenproof plates but don't allow them to overlap or they will cook unevenly. Brush the fish slices with more olive oil or melted butter, season with salt and freshly ground pepper and sprinkle each plate with a little of the freshly chopped herbs. Put the plates in the preheated oven and cook for 3 minutes; you might like to check after 2 minutes if the slices are exceptionally thin. The fish is cooked when it looks opaque.

Rush it to the table, serve with crusty white bread, a good green salad and a glass of white wine.

VARIATION
Ring the changes with a little chopped chilli, coriander or freshly roasted crushed spices, such as cumin or coriander.

PENNE WITH FRESH SALMON & garden peas

Serves 4

Sanford Allen, a charismatic American violinist friend gave me this fresh-tasting pasta recipe originally. Ideally use peas fresh from the garden, but good-quality frozen peas also work well. Sometimes I omit the lemon juice and add a good dash of cream instead.

225g penne

225g peas

225g fresh wild or organic salmon or
   half smoked and half fresh salmon

3 tablespoons extra virgin olive oil

1 large garlic clove, finely chopped

a pinch of sugar

15g salted butter, melted

2–3 tablespoons freshly chopped dill and flat-leaf
   parsley, plus extra to garnish

freshly squeezed juice of ½ lemon

approx. 1–2 tablespoons freshly chopped
   flat-leaf parsley or dill

salt and freshly ground black pepper

Bring 4 litres of water and 2 tablespoons of salt to the boil in a large saucepan. Cook the penne for 10–12 minutes until al dente. Blanch the peas in boiling water for 2–3 minutes, drain. Frozen peas may take a minute more to cook.

Skin the salmon and cut into 1cm cubes. Heat 1 tablespoon of olive oil in a sauté pan, add the garlic, toss over a medium heat for a minute or two, then add the salmon and toss gently until it changes colour. Add the blanched peas. Season with sugar, salt and freshly ground pepper.

Drain the penne and toss in the remaining olive oil and the melted butter. Add the salmon mixture, dill, parsley and freshly squeezed lemon juice, toss gently and season to taste. Transfer to a hot serving dish, sprinkle with lots of chopped dill and parsley and enjoy immediately.

SMOKED & FRESH SALMON FISHCAKES
with parsley butter

Serves 10

Fishcakes and fish pie make the yummiest suppers. Here, I'm using both fresh and smoked salmon, but of course you can use a variety of other fish. A big dollop of aioli or tartare sauce is pretty irresistible too.

285g salmon

450g unpeeled 'old' potatoes, such as
   Golden Wonders or Kerr's Pinks

1 organic egg, beaten

30–55g salted butter

1 tablespoon freshly chopped parsley

2 tablespoons freshly chopped coriander

2 tablespoons chopped spring onions

55g smoked salmon, diced into 3mm cubes

creamy milk (optional)

seasoned plain flour

beaten egg, for coating

fresh white breadcrumbs or panko crumbs

extra virgin olive oil or clarified butter (page 185),
   for frying

salt and freshly ground black pepper

For the parsley butter

50g butter

4 teaspoons finely chopped parsley

a few drops of freshly squeezed lemon juice

To make the parsley butter, cream the butter and stir in the parsley and a few drops of lemon juice at a time. Roll into butter pats or form into a roll and wrap in greaseproof paper or tin foil, twisting each end so that it looks like a cracker. Refrigerate to harden.

Cook the salmon in boiling salted water for 5–8 minutes depending on size, allow to cool. Skin and remove the bones.

Meanwhile cook the potatoes in their jackets, pull off the peel and mash right away. Add the beaten egg, butter, chopped herbs, spring onions, flaked fresh salmon and diced smoked salmon. Season with lots of salt and freshly ground pepper, adding a few drops of creamy milk if the mixture is too stiff.

Shape into fish cakes about 7.5cm in diameter and 2.5cm thick. Dip first in well seasoned flour, then the beaten egg and finally in breadcrumbs.

Melt some extra virgin olive oil or clarified butter in a frying pan over a gentle heat. Fry the salmon and potato cakes until golden on one side, flip over and cook on the other side for 4–5 minutes; they should be crusty and golden.

Serve on hot plates with a blob of parsley butter melting on top, or a dollop of homemade tartare sauce or aioli (page 32).

SMOKED HADDOCK WITH PARMESAN

Avoid the scary bright orange smoked haddock, instead seek out an artisan smoked product or better still smoke your own fish in a tin biscuit box over a low flame on your stove, it's so easy and such fun. If you surround the fish with some mashed potato, supper's ready. Follow with a salad of organic leaves.

700g smoked haddock, ling or hake

600ml whole milk

a few slices of carrot

a few slices of onion

bouquet garni

50g roux (page 76)

2 tablespoons freshly chopped parsley

110g grated cheese (preferably Parmesan
    but mature Cheddar would be wonderful too)

buttered crumbs (page 96)

1kg mashed potato

Preheat the oven to 180°C/gas mark 4.

Cut the smoked fish into portions weighing 50–110g and arrange in a wide sauté pan.

Put the cold milk into a saucepan with the carrot, onion and bouquet garni. Bring slowly to the boil and simmer for 3–4 minutes; remove from the heat and leave to infuse for 10–15 minutes. Strain. Cover the fish with the flavoured milk and simmer for 3–6 minutes or until just cooked, depending on the thickness of the fish. Transfer the fish to an ovenproof serving dish with a slotted spoon.

Bring the milk back to the boil, thicken with roux to a light coating consistency, add the parsley and half the cheese, taste and spoon over the haddock in the dish. Sprinkle with a mixture of buttered crumbs and the remaining grated cheese. Pipe mashed potato around the outside of the dish. (You can prepare ahead to this point).

Bake in the oven for 15–20 minutes or until the top is crisp and bubbly and the potato edges are golden, then serve with a lightly dressed salad of organic leaves.

COD, HAKE OR HADDOCK
with Dijon mustard sauce

Serves 6

Virtually any round fish may be used in this recipe so choose from cod, hake, ling, haddock, grey sea mullet or pollock. This recipe is another gem that you'll return to over and over again.

55g salted butter

225g chopped onions

900g fresh cod fillets

600ml whole milk

50ml whipping cream

30g plain flour

2–3 tablespoons Dijon or English mustard

1 tablespoon freshly chopped parsley

790g Duchesse potato (optional)

sea salt and freshly ground black pepper

Melt the butter and sweat the onions in a covered saucepan until golden brown.

Skin the cod and cut into portions. Season with salt and freshly ground pepper. Put into a wide sauté pan or frying pan, cover with the milk and cream, bring to the boil and simmer gently for 4–6 minutes, depending on the thickness of the fish. Remove the fish carefully to a serving dish.

Add the flour to the onions, stir and cook for 2 minutes. Add in the hot fishy milk, bring back to the boil and simmer for 3–4 minutes until a light coating consistency. Add the mustard and chopped parsley, season to taste, then pour over the fish and serve with your choice of vegetables.

Duchesse Potato may be piped around this dish. You can leave it to cool and reheat later in a moderate oven at 180°C/gas mark 4, for about 20 minutes.

VARIATIONS

⌁ Sprinkle 110–170g of sliced sautéed mushrooms over or under the fish before saucing.

⌁ Sweat 450g of finely sliced leeks in 30g of salted butter in a covered casserole over a gentle heat and use instead of mushrooms.

⌁ Peel and sweat 75–110g chopped cucumber in 15–30g of salted butter with a dessertspoon of dill in a covered casserole over a gentle heat. Use instead of mushrooms and omit mustard from the sauce.

⌁ Put a layer of tomato fondue (page 127) on or over the fish and proceed as in the master recipe (omit mustard from the sauce).

⌁ Put a layer of peperonata under or over the fish and proceed as in the master recipe (omit mustard from the sauce).

vegetables

ASPARAGUS & SPRING ONION TART

In Ireland asparagus is only in season during the month of May – you may be fortunate enough to get a few early spears towards the end of April, and a few stragglers in early June, but it's best to stop cutting it then to allow the remaining spears to flower and the fern to feed the plant for the following year. This tart is therefore a seasonal luxury and simply not worth making with asparagus that has been flown halfway across the world. The pastry case needs to be well cooked before the filling is added, cook it on a lower rack, rather than too high in the oven.

For the shortcrust pastry

110g plain flour

50g salted butter

water or a small organic, free-range egg (you will not need all of the egg)

For the filling

15g salted butter

1 tablespoon extra virgin olive oil

250g onions, finely chopped (I use about half spring onion complete with green tops and half white onion)

150g asparagus, trimmed and with ends peeled

3 organic, free-range eggs

110ml cream

110g Cheddar cheese, grated

sea salt and freshly ground black pepper

Preheat the oven to 180°C/gas mark 4.

First make the shortcrust pastry. Sift the flour into a bowl and rub in the butter until the mixture resembles coarse breadcrumbs. Mix in enough water or a mixture of beaten egg and water to bind the pastry, be careful not to make the pastry too sticky. Chill for 15 minutes.

Roll out the pastry into a circle large enough to line an 18cm quiche tin, not more than 3mm thick. Line the pastry case with greaseproof paper and fill to the top with dried beans. Bake blind for about 20 minutes. Remove the beans and paper, eggwash the base and return to the oven for 3–4 minutes. This seals the pastry and helps to avoid a 'soggy bottom'.

Next make the filling. Melt the butter, add the olive oil and chopped onions; sweat with a good pinch of salt until soft but not coloured.

Cook the asparagus in boiling salted water for 3–4 minutes until al dente, then drain. Refresh in cold water and then drain again. When it is cool enough to handle, cut into 1cm pieces. Whisk the eggs in a bowl; add the cream, sweated onion, almost all of the cheese and the cooked asparagus. (You may want to save a few of the tips to arrange on top.) Season with salt and freshly ground pepper. Pour into the pastry case, sprinkle the remaining cheese on top and bake for 40–45 minutes or until a skewer inserted into the centre just comes out clean. Serve warm, with a good green salad.

COURGETTE & BASIL LASAGNE

Serves 6–8

When you consider making lasagne is just a technique then you can ring the changes with all manner of fillings. This simple vegetarian version is unexpectedly delicious. I sometimes use annual marjoram instead of basil with equally delicious results.

9 sheets of lasagne (choose the thinnest lasagne possible)

900g courgettes, thinly sliced and cooked for 3–4 minutes in extra virgin olive oil

150g Parmesan cheese, preferably Parmigiano Reggiano, freshly grated

20–30 basil leaves, depending on size

sea salt and freshly ground black pepper

For the Béchamel sauce

900ml whole milk

a few slices of carrot

a few slices of onion

3 small sprigs of thyme

3 small sprigs of parsley

9 peppercorns

105g roux (page 76)

Preheat the oven to 180°C/gas mark 4.

Blanch the lasagne in boiling salted water for a minute or so if it is homemade, or according to the directions on the packet. Drain and lay on a tea towel until needed.

To make the Béchamel sauce, put the milk into a saucepan with the carrot, onion, peppercorns, thyme and parsley. Bring to the boil, simmer for 4–5 minutes, remove from the heat and leave to infuse for 10 minutes.

Strain out the vegetables and herbs, bring the milk back to the boil and whisk in the roux to thicken to a light coating consistency. Allow to bubble gently for 4–5 minutes. Season to taste.

Taste the cooked courgettes and make sure they are delicious and well-seasoned. Spread a little Béchamel sauce on the base of a lightly buttered 25.5 x 30.5cm gratin dish, sprinkle with a little grated Parmesan, cover with strips of lasagne, more Béchamel sauce, a sprinkling of Parmesan, half the courgettes and a layer of basil leaves. Next add another layer of lasagne and repeat the previous layer. Cover the final layer of lasagne with sauce and a good sprinkling of Parmesan. (Make sure all the lasagne is coated with sauce.)

Bake for 10–15 minutes or until golden and bubbly on top. If possible, leave to stand for 5–10 minutes before cutting to allow the layers to compact. Serve garnished with extra basil leaves and a good green salad.

PIZZA with broccoli, mozzarella & garlic

Makes 1
Serves 1–2

Philip Dennhardt launched the pop-up Saturday Pizzas at the Ballymaloe Cookery School in 2008 and quickly gained a cult following. I find it convenient to pop a few rolled out uncooked pizza bases in the freezer when using this dough. You can take one out, put the topping on and slide it straight in the oven. What could be easier! This dough also makes delicious white yeast bread which you can shape into rolls, loaves and plaits.

semolina flour, to sprinkle

2 tablespoons extra virgin olive oil

2–3 garlic cloves, cut into thin slivers

110g calabrese, green broccoli or romanesco, cooked

75g buffalo mozzarella, torn

15g Parmesan or aged Coolea cheese, grated

flaky sea salt

chilli oil (optional)

For the pizza dough

680g strong white flour or 600g strong white flour and 100g rye flour

2 level teaspoons salt

15g granulated sugar

50g butter

7g packet fast-acting yeast

2–4 tablespoons olive oil, plus extra for brushing

450ml–500ml lukewarm water, more if necessary

To make the dough, sift the flour into a large, wide mixing bowl and add the salt and sugar. Rub in the butter and yeast and mix all the ingredients together thoroughly. Make a well in the centre of the dry ingredients, add the oil and most of the lukewarm water. Mix to form a loose dough. You can add more water or flour if needed. Turn the dough onto a lightly floured worktop, cover and leave to relax for about 5 minutes.

Knead the dough for 8–9 minutes or until smooth and springy (if kneading in a food mixer with a dough hook, 5 minutes is usually long enough). Leave the dough to relax again for about 10 minutes, then shape and measure into 8 equal balls of dough, each weighing about 150g. Lightly brush the balls of dough with olive oil. If you have time, put the oiled balls of dough into a plastic bag and chill. The dough will be easier to handle when cold but can be used immediately.

Preheat the oven to 240°C/gas mark 9.

On a well-floured work surface, roll out a ball of pizza dough to a 25cm disc. Sprinkle a little semolina all over the surface of the pizza paddle, if using, and put the pizza base on top.

Brush the edges of the dough with extra virgin olive oil. Sprinkle thin slivers of garlic over the base, arrange the broccoli florets on top and sprinkle the mozzarella and grated Parmesan. Drizzle with extra virgin olive oil and season with flaky sea salt. Slide off the paddle onto a hot baking tray and bake for 5–8 minutes. Drizzle with chilli oil if you wish and serve immediately.

SUMMER HEIRLOOM TOMATO & BASIL TART

Serves 6–8

This tart is only sublime when the tomatoes are superbly ripe and the basil is in season, otherwise it's probably better to make something else. I love it made with a mixture of the heirloom tomatoes we grow in the greenhouse but any variety of ripe, juicy red ones will be good too.

For the rich shortcrust pastry
175g plain flour
75g salted butter
1 organic, free-range egg yolk
2 tablespoons water
For the filling
2 organic, free-range eggs
75ml double cream
85g grated Emmental or Gruyére cheese

25g freshly grated Parmesan, preferably
    Parmigiano Reggiano
275g very ripe heirloom tomatoes
pinch of granulated sugar
4–5 large basil leaves, torn
1 tablespoon finely snipped chives
sea salt and freshly ground black pepper
balsamic vinegar (optional)

Preheat the oven to 180°C/gas mark 4.

First make the pastry. Sift the flour into a wide bowl and rub in the butter until it resembles coarse breadcrumbs. Mix the egg yolk and water together and use to bind the pastry. Add a little more water if necessary, but don't make it too sticky. Chill for 15 minutes, then roll out to line a 20.5cm tart tin to a thickness of about 3mm. Line with greaseproof paper and fill to the top with dried beans. Rest for 15 minutes and then bake for 20 minutes. Remove the beans and paper and save for another time. Leave to cool.

Next make the filling. Whisk the eggs with the cream in a bowl, add the cheese, season with salt and freshly ground pepper to taste. Scald and peel the tomatoes and cut into 5mm rings, season with sugar, salt and freshly ground pepper and a dash of balsamic vinegar if you have a nice bottle to hand. Put a few tablespoons of the custard into the pastry case and then a layer of tomato rings. Sprinkle on a layer of torn basil leaves and chopped chives. Spoon in the remaining custard and top with the remaining seasoned tomato rings. Sprinkle with a few flakes of sea salt.

Bake for about 30 minutes or until the tart is just set and golden on top. Serve with a salad of organic leaves.

MAC 'N' CHEESE

Serves 6

What's not to love about mac 'n' cheese? It's just about everyone's favourite comfort food. Gorgeous in its original form, but you can vary it almost infinitely – lobster mac 'n' cheese, or add smoked mackerel, eel or salmon, or just some streaky bacon.

225g macaroni

50g salted butter

50g plain flour

850ml whole milk, boiling

¼ teaspoon Dijon or English mustard

1 tablespoon freshly chopped flat-leaf parsley
  (optional)

150g grated mature Cheddar cheese, or a mixture
  of Gruyère, Parmesan and Cheddar, plus an
  extra 25g grated cheese for sprinkling on top

sea salt and freshly ground black pepper

In a large saucepan bring 3.4 litres of water to the boil and add 2 teaspoons of salt. Sprinkle in the macaroni and stir to make sure it doesn't stick together. Cook for 10–15 minutes until just soft. Drain well.

Meanwhile, melt the butter in a saucepan, add the flour and cook over a medium heat, stirring occasionally for 1–2 minutes. Remove from the heat. Whisk in the milk gradually; return to the boil, stirring all the time. Add the mustard, parsley, if using, and cheese, season with salt and freshly ground pepper to taste. Add the cooked macaroni, bring back to the boil, season to taste. Macaroni cheese reheats very successfully provided the pasta is not overcooked in the first place.

Turn into a 1.1-litre pie dish, sprinkle grated cheese over the top. Reheat in the oven at 180°C/ gas mark 4 for 15–20 minutes. It is very good served with cold meat, particularly ham.

VARIATIONS

⌒ *Macaroni Cheese with Smoked Salmon or Smoked Mackerel* Add 225g smoked salmon or mackerel dice to the mac 'n' cheese.

⌒ *Macaroni Cheese with Mushrooms & Courgettes* Add 225g of sliced sautéed mushrooms and 225g sliced courgettes cooked in olive oil with a little garlic and marjoram or basil and add to the mac 'n' cheese. Toss gently, turn into a hot serving dish and scatter with grated cheese – delish.

⌒ *Macaroni Cheese with Chorizo* Add 225g diced chorizo and lots of chopped parsley to the mac 'n' cheese as you put it into the dish.

GRATIN OF LEEKS MORNAY

Serves 8

A comforting supper dish, I sometimes wrap each leek in a slice of ham before coating in the mornay sauce, as Maman did when I was an au pair in France. Chicory may be substituted for leeks, and very delicious they are too.

8 leeks

600ml whole milk

a few slices of carrot and onion

5 peppercorns

roux (page 76)

1 sprig of thyme and parsley

¼ teaspoon Dijon mustard

140–170g grated Cheddar cheese or

   85g grated Parmesan cheese

buttered crumbs (page 96 – optional)

sea salt and freshly ground black pepper

Preheat the oven to 180°C/gas mark 4.

Trim most of the green part off the leeks (use in the stock pot). Leave the white parts whole, slit the top and wash well under cold running water. Cook in a little boiling salted water in a covered saucepan for about 15 minutes until just tender.

Meanwhile, put the cold milk into a saucepan with the carrot, onion, peppercorns, thyme and parsley. Bring to the boil, simmer for 5 minutes, remove from the heat and leave to infuse for 10 minutes. Strain out the vegetables, return to the boil and thicken with roux to a light coating consistency. Add the mustard and two-thirds of the grated cheese. Season with salt and freshly ground pepper to taste.

Drain the leeks well, arrange in an ovenproof serving dish, coat with the sauce and sprinkle with the remaining grated cheese mixed with a few buttered crumbs. Bake for about 15 minutes until golden and bubbly.

CAULIFLOWER CHEESE

Serves 6–8

Ah, cauliflower cheese, who doesn't love a big dish of bubbly cauliflower cheese with a layer of golden cheese melting on top? Make more than you need, save the cauliflower cooking water and transform any leftovers into the most delicious soup that will have all the family begging for more. Follow the recipe below but instead of browning in the oven or under the grill, liquidise the lot with any leftover cauliflower cooking water and 850ml light chicken stock to make a nice consistency. Season the soup to taste and serve with croutons, cubes of diced Cheddar cheese and freshly chopped parsley.

1 cauliflower with green leaves
pinch of salt
freshly chopped flat-leaf parsley, to garnish
For the cheese sauce
600ml whole milk with a dash of cream
½ onion, cut in chunks
1 small carrot, cut in chunks

6 black peppercorns
a sprig of thyme and some parsley stalks
roux (page 76)
150g grated cheese, such as Cheddar or better still
   a mixture of Gruyére, Parmesan and Cheddar
½ teaspoon Dijon mustard
sea salt and freshly ground black pepper

Preheat the oven to 230°C/gas mark 8.

Prepare and cook the cauliflower. Remove the outer leaves and wash both the cauliflower and the leaves well. Put no more than 2.5cm of water in a saucepan just large enough to take the cauliflower; add a little salt. Chop the leaves into small pieces and cut the cauliflower in quarters or eighths; place the cauliflower on top of the green leaves in the saucepan, cover with a lid and simmer for 8–10 minutes until cooked. Test by piercing the stalk with a knife – they should be tender right through.

Meanwhile, make the cheese sauce. Put the cold milk into a saucepan with the onion, carrot, peppercorns and herbs. Bring to the boil, simmer for 3–4 minutes, remove from the heat and leave to infuse for 10 minutes.

Strain out the vegetables, return the milk to the boil and whisk in the roux until it reaches a light coating consistency. Add most of the grated cheese (save enough to sprinkle over the dish) and mustard. Season to taste. Spoon the sauce over the cauliflower and sprinkle with the remaining grated cheese. The dish may be prepared ahead to this point.

Put into the preheated oven or under the grill to brown. If the cauliflower cheese is allowed to cool completely it will take 20–25 minutes to reheat in the oven at 180°C/gas mark 4. Serve sprinkled with the parsley.

SUMMER FRITTATA with courgette, basil & marjoram

Serves 2

This is one of the flat Mediterranean omelettes that are simply divine for a summer lunch. Somehow one bite transports you to the magical world of Provence. It is a feast when the courgettes are fresh and crisp and no longer than 15cm. Use a mixture of green and golden, I urge you to grow a plant or two yourself even if it's only in a couple of containers in your backyard. They produce a bumper crop and you'll also have the golden flowers to use in myriad ways in salads, fritters or even stuffed with fish or shellfish.

285g crisp courgettes, not more than 15cm in length, plus blossoms, to garnish (optional)

5 tablespoons extra virgin olive oil

6 organic, free-range eggs

1 dessertspoon annual marjoram or fresh torn basil leaves

2 dessertspoons freshly chopped flat-leaf parsley

6–8 black Niçoise olives, to garnish

flaky sea salt and freshly ground black pepper

Slice the unpeeled courgettes into very thin rounds. Heat 2 tablespoons of extra virgin olive oil in a pan, add the courgettes. Season with flaky salt and freshly ground pepper and cook for 2–3 minutes until al dente. Drain.

Thoroughly whisk the eggs in a bowl, season with salt and freshly ground pepper, add most of the freshly chopped herbs and finally the courgettes. Heat 2 tablespoons of extra virgin olive oil in a 12.5cm or 15cm non-stick frying pan over a high heat, pour in the omelette mixture then reduce the heat to medium and continue to cook until the omelette is set and golden on the bottom but still a little juicy on top. Alternatively, start by cooking on the hob, then transfer to an oven preheated to 160°C/gas mark 3 and bake until set.

Place a hot plate over the top of the pan and with the help of a tea towel quickly turn it upside down so the omelette ends up on the plate golden side upwards. (Easier said than done!) Drizzle with the remaining olive oil and scatter a few courgette blossoms, black olives and the remaining herbs over the top. Serve warm or at room temperature with a salad of organic leaves and summer herbs.

TOMATO & PESTO OMELETTE

Serves 1

An omelette is the ultimate fast food but many a travesty is served up in its name. The secret is to have the pan hot enough and to use clarified butter if at all possible. Ordinary butter will burn if your pan is as hot as it ought to be. The omelette should be made in half the time it takes to read this recipe – your first may not be a joy to behold but persevere, practice makes perfect! The filling can be varied endlessly, depending on what you have to hand.

2 organic, free-range eggs

1 dessertspoon water or whole milk

1 dessertspoon clarified butter (page 185) or olive oil

2 tablespoons tomato fondue (see below)

1 tablespoon wild garlic or basil pesto

sea salt and freshly ground black pepper

For the tomato fondue

2 tablespoons extra virgin olive oil

110g sliced onions

1 garlic clove, crushed

900g very ripe tomatoes, sliced, or 2 x 400g cans chopped tomatoes

granulated sugar, to taste

1 tablespoon of any of the following: freshly chopped mint, thyme, parsley, lemon balm, marjoram or torn basil

To make the tomato fondue, heat the oil in a stainless steel sauté pan or casserole. Add the sliced onions and garlic and toss until coated, then cover and sweat over a gentle heat for about 10 minutes until soft but not coloured. Add the tomatoes with all the juice and season with sugar (canned tomatoes need lots of sugar because of their high acidity), salt and freshly ground pepper. Add a generous sprinkling of herbs or just basil. Cover and cook for 10–20 minutes or until the tomato softens, uncover and reduce a little.

To make the omelette, warm a plate in the oven, it mustn't be too hot. All your ingredients must be ready and to hand. The tomato fondue needs to be bubbling in a pot.

Whisk the eggs with the water or milk in a bowl with a fork until thoroughly mixed but not too fluffy. Season with salt and pepper. Put the warm plate beside the cooker. Heat a 23cm omelette pan over a high heat and add the clarified butter or olive oil. As soon as it sizzles, pour the eggs into the pan. It will start to cook immediately so quickly pull the edges of the omelette towards the centre with a metal spoon or spatula, tilting the pan so that the uncooked egg runs to the sides. Continue for a few seconds until most of the egg is set and will not run any more, then spoon the hot tomato fondue along the centre of the omelette and drizzle a little pesto over it.

Immediately, flip the edge just below the handle of the pan into the centre to cover the filling, then hold the pan almost perpendicular over the plate so that the omelette will fold over again, then half roll half slide the omelette onto the plate so that it lands folded in three.

PASTA WITH BROAD BEANS pancetta & olive oil

Serves 4

Broad beans are well worth growing if you have a little space. They need to be absolutely fresh otherwise they can taste dull and mealy as the sugars turn to starch within a few hours. So for most people it's impossible to find them freshly harvested at the peak of perfection unless you grow them or are friends with a gardener, or have a terrific farmers' market close by.

450g pasta, such as spaghetti, fettuccine or
    tagliatelle
110g pancetta or mild very thinly sliced
fat streaky bacon, diced
3 garlic cloves, crushed
1kg broad beans, shelled, blanched and refreshed
    (should yield 225–350g beans)

3 tablespoons extra virgin olive oil
1 tablespoon salted butter
2 tablespoons flat-leaf parsley, coarsely chopped
freshly grated Parmesan cheese, such as
    Parmigiano Reggiano or Grana Padana

In a large saucepan bring 4.8 litres of water to the boil and add 1 generous tablespoon of salt. Cook the pasta until it is almost al dente, about 5–8 minutes, depending on the type of pasta.

Meanwhile, bring 600ml water to a rolling boil in a saucepan, then add 1 teaspoon of salt. Add the broad beans and cook for 3–6 minutes depending on size and freshness. Drain, refresh quickly and slip the beans out of their shells.

Meanwhile, heat most of the extra virgin olive oil in a frying pan, add the pancetta or diced bacon and cook until crispish. Add the crushed garlic, cook for a minute or so, then add the broad beans. When the pasta is just cooked, drain immediately, toss in a little butter and extra virgin olive oil and mix with the broad beans and pancetta. Toss again, transfer to hot plates. Shower with the chopped parsley and freshly grated cheese and serve immediately.

THE PERFECT RISOTTO

Serves 6

Risotto is one of my top ten dishes. No child should leave home without being able to whip up a gorgeous risotto, one of the easiest ways to win friends and influence people. You'll need Carnaroli, Arborio or Vilano Nano rice. The technique is altogether different to the Indian pilaffs and for perfection it should be served the moment it is cooked. You can also add some dry white wine to the rice and reduce before adding the stock.

1–1.3 litres homemade chicken or vegetable stock

85g salted butter

225g mushrooms, sliced, porcini or cremini are particularly delicious

2 tablespoons extra virgin olive oil

1 onion, finely chopped

400g Arborio, Carnaroli or Vilano nano rice

55g freshly grated Parmesan cheese, preferably Parmigiano Reggiano

sea salt and freshly ground black pepper

Bring the stock to the boil, reduce the heat and keep it simmering.

To cook the mushrooms, melt 30g butter in a saucepan, just as it foams add the mushrooms, season with salt and freshly ground pepper, reduce the heat and cook long and slowly until the mushrooms are dark and concentrated in flavour. This method of cooking mushrooms transforms their flavour and makes them taste like wild mushrooms.

Melt 30g butter in a heavy-bottomed saucepan with the extra virgin olive oil, add the onion and sweat over a gentle heat for 4–5 minutes until soft but not coloured. Add the rice and stir until well coated (so far the technique is the same as for a pilaff and this is where people become confused). Cook for a minute or so and then add a ladleful of the simmering stock, stir continuously and as soon as the liquid is absorbed add another ladleful of stock. Continue to cook, stirring continuously. The heat should be brisk, but on the other hand if it's too hot the rice will be soft outside but still chewy inside. If it's too slow, the rice will be gluey. It's difficult to know which is worse, so the trick is to regulate the heat so that the rice bubbles continuously. The risotto should take about 25–30 minutes to cook. When it has been cooking for about 20 minutes, add in the cooked mushrooms and from there on add the stock about half a ladle at a time.

The risotto is done when the rice is cooked but is still ever so slightly al dente. It should be soft and creamy and quite loose, rather than thick. The moment you are happy with the texture, stir in the remaining butter and Parmesan cheese, taste and add more salt if necessary. Serve immediately. Risotto should not hang about otherwise it will become thick and gloopy.

LEEK, POTATO & CHEDDAR CHEESE PIE

Serves 8

Homely and comforting, a super delicious autumn or winter supper dish. It also makes a delicious gratin to serve with a fine roast or a steak.

450g 'old' potatoes, such as Golden Wonders
    or Kerr's Pinks
450g leeks
50g salted butter
600ml Cheddar cheese sauce (page 124)
½ garlic clove, crushed

2 tablespoons grated Cheddar cheese
    buttered crumbs (optional – page 96)
sea salt and freshly ground black pepper

Preheat the oven to 180°C/gas mark 4.

Cook the potatoes in boiling salted water. Cut the green parts off the leeks and save for the stockpot. Wash the white parts well and cut into 1cm rounds. Melt the butter in a casserole, toss in the leeks, season with salt and freshly ground pepper, cover and cook for 5–6 minutes over a very low heat. Turn off the heat and let them continue to cook in the covered pot in the residual heat while you make the cheese sauce, adding the crushed garlic clove; it should be a light coating consistency.

When the potatoes are cooked, peel and cut into 1cm cubes and mix gently with the leeks and cheese sauce. Turn into a 1.1-litre pie dish. Sprinkle generously with grated cheese or a mixture of buttered crumbs and grated cheese.

Bake for about 20 minutes until golden and bubbly on top.

TAGLIATELLE WITH CREAM & ASPARAGUS

Serves 4

Asparagus is in season in Ireland during the month of May. We grow an old variety of green asparagus called Martha Washington, it's heaven… This dish is wickedly rich but utterly delicious once a year!

225g fresh asparagus
225g tagliatelle or taglierini, preferably fresh
 and homemade
30g salted butter
170g best-quality cream

55g freshly grated Parmesan cheese
 (Parmigiano Reggiano is best)
a little freshly grated nutmeg
sea salt and freshly ground black pepper

Snap off the root end of the asparagus where it breaks naturally. Cook the asparagus in boiling salted water for 3–4 minutes until al dente. Drain and refresh in cold water, drain again and save.

Bring 4 litres of water to a good rolling boil, add 2 tablespoons of salt and drop in the tagliatelle, cover the pan just for a few seconds until the water comes back to the boil. Cook the tagliatelle until barely al dente (remember it will cook a little more in the pan). Homemade tagliatelle will take only 1–2 minutes whereas dried pasta will take considerably longer, 10–12 minutes depending on the brand. (Save a little of the pasta cooking water in case the sauce needs to be loosened.)

Cut the asparagus into thin slices at an angle (no thicker than 5mm). Melt the butter in a wide saucepan, add half the cream, simmer for a couple of minutes just until the cream thickens slightly, add the asparagus, the hot, drained tagliatelle, remaining cream and the freshly grated cheese. Season with a little grated nutmeg, sea salt and freshly ground pepper. Toss briefly just enough to coat the pasta and season to taste. Serve immediately.

PROVENÇALE BEAN STEW

Serves 6–8

This is a delicious rustic bean stew, cheap to make yet wonderfully filling and nutritious, and a particularly good dish for vegetarians. Do not add the salt to the beans until near the end of the cooking time, otherwise they seem to harden. Add some Aleppo pepper or a few pepper flakes if you fancy, and of course you can add some spicy merguez sausages or chorizo if you wish. If this bean stew is being eaten without meat, then rice should be eaten in the same meal in order to get maximum nutritional benefit from the beans.

110g dried haricot beans

110g kidney beans

110g black-eyed beans

3 small carrots

3 onions

3–4 bouquet garni

2 tablespoons extra virgin olive oil

225g sliced onions

1 large red pepper, cored, deseeded and sliced

1 large green pepper, cored, deseeded and sliced

2 garlic cloves, crushed

1 x 400g can tomatoes or 450g peeled, very ripe
   tomatoes, chopped

2 tablespoons concentrated tomato purée
   (page 18)

1 tablespoon freshly chopped marjoram,
   thyme or basil

pinch of granulated sugar

55g black Kalamata olives

2 tablespoons freshly chopped flat-leaf parsley or
   coriander, plus extra to garnish

sea salt and freshly ground black pepper and sugar

The day before cooking, pick over the beans, in three separate bowls, cover with plenty of cold water and leave overnight (soak each type of bean separately). Next day, drain the beans, place in three separate saucepans and cover with fresh cold water. Add a carrot, an onion and a bouquet garni to each pan. Bring to the boil, boil rapidly for 10 minutes, then cover and simmer until almost tender. The cooking time varies according to the variety and age of the beans, so for this reason it is better to cook the beans separately and mix them later. Add a pinch of salt towards the end of cooking.

When the beans are tender but not mushy, strain and reserve 300ml of the liquid and discard the vegetables and bouquet garni. Heat the oil in a casserole and sweat the sliced onions over a low heat for about 5 minutes until sweet and slightly golden. Add the peppers and garlic, cover and continue to sweat gently for 10 minutes. Add the tomatoes with their juice, tomato purée, marjoram, beans, remaining bouquet garni, reserved cooking liquid, salt, freshly ground pepper and a pinch of sugar. Cover and simmer for about 20 minutes or until the beans and peppers are cooked. Five minutes before the end of the cooking time, add the olives and freshly chopped parsley or coriander. Remove the bouquet garni and season to taste. Serve with extra chopped parsley to garnish.

POTATO, CARROT & CAULIFLOWER CURRY
with coriander & toasted almonds

Serves 4

Sophie Grigson, the bubbly cook of the many earrings, made this exceptionally delicious vegetable curry when she was guest chef at the school in 1993 and we've been enjoying it ever since.

200g small new potatoes, or waxy salad potatoes

200g cauliflower florets

200g carrots, sliced at an angle

4 green cardamon pods

1 tablespoon coriander seeds

2 teaspoons cumin seeds

2 dried red chillis, deseeded and broken into pieces

4 tablespoons desiccated coconut
  (we use frozen nowadays)

1 scant teaspoon grated fresh ginger

250ml thick organic natural yogurt or labneh

45g salted butter

2 tablespoons extra virgin olive oil

1 small onion, grated

2 tablespoons water

30g toasted flaked almonds, to garnish

1 tablespoon freshly chopped coriander leaves,
  to garnish

Boil the potatoes in their jackets in boiling salted water until just tender. Peel off the skin and halve or quarter depending on size. Steam or boil the cauliflower until barely cooked. Drain well. Steam or boil the carrots until just cooked.

Split the cardamon pods and extract the seeds. Mix with the coriander and cumin seeds. Dry-fry in a heavy pan over a high heat until they smell aromatic. Tip into a bowl. Dry-fry the chilli (which makes it easier to grind), add the coconut and fry until pale golden, then mix with the spices. Cool, grind to a powder and mix with the ginger and yogurt.

Melt the butter with the oil in a sauté or frying pan, and cook the potatoes, cauliflower and carrots briskly until patched with brown. Set aside. Add the onion to the fat and fry until golden brown, then stir in the thick yogurt mixture a tablespoon at a time. Cook, stirring for 2 minutes, then stir in the water, followed by the potatoes and cauliflower. Stir until piping hot. Serve sprinkled with toasted almonds and fresh coriander leaves.

BAKED EGGS WITH MANY GOOD THINGS

Serves 4

Great as a starter or a snack, there are infinite variations on the theme but the eggs must be super-fresh and the cream rich.

15g salted butter
6–8 tablespoons rich Jersey cream
4 fresh organic, free-range eggs
flaky sea salt and freshly ground black pepper

Lightly butter four small ramekins. Heat the cream; when it is hot, spoon about 1 tablespoon into each ramekin and break an egg into the cream. Season with flaky sea salt and freshly ground pepper. Spoon the remaining cream over the top of the eggs. Place the ramekins in a bain-marie of hot water, cover with foil or a lid and bring to simmering point on the hob. Continue to cook either gently on the hob or in the oven at 180°C/gas mark 4 for about 10 minutes for a soft egg, 12 minutes for a medium egg. Serve immediately.

VARIATIONS

⌐ *Baked Eggs with Cheese* Sprinkle ½–1 tablespoon of finely grated Parmesan, Gruyère or Cheddar cheese or a mixture of all three on top of each egg. Bake uncovered in a bain-marie in the oven if you prefer.

⌐ *Baked Eggs with Tomato Fondue* Put 1 tablespoon of Tomato fondue (page 127) underneath each egg in the ramekins. Proceed as in the master recipe, with or without the cheese.

⌐ *Baked Eggs with Smoked Salmon or Mackerel* Put 1 tablespoon of chopped smoked salmon or flaked smoked mackerel in the base of each ramekin. Add 1–2 tablespoons of freshly chopped flat-leaf parsley to the cream and proceed as in the master recipe.

⌐ *Baked Eggs with Fresh Herbs & Dijon Mustard* Use 3 tablespoons in total of flat-leaf parsley, tarragon, chives and chervil. Mix 2 teaspoons of mustard and 3 tablespoons of freshly chopped herbs into the cream and proceed as for the master recipe.

⌐ *Baked Eggs with Yogurt & Paprika Oil* Put a dollop of natural yogurt on top just before serving. Drizzle with paprika oil (just gently heat 1 teaspoon of sweet or smoked paprika in 4 tablespoons of extra virgin olive oil).

LEEKS WITH YELLOW PEPPERS & MARJORAM

Serves 6

I love to roast or chargrill leeks but this braised version is also irresistible served as a side dish or light lunch in crispy shortcrust tartlets or in filo triangles as a starter.

6 young leeks, about 2.5cm in diameter

3 yellow peppers

15g salted butter

1 tablespoon extra virgin olive oil

1–2 tablespoons freshly chopped annual marjoram or a mixture of parsley, basil and marjoram

sea salt and freshly ground black pepper

Wash and slice the leeks into 5mm rounds. Quarter the peppers and cut into 5mm thick slices on the bias. Melt the butter and olive oil in a heavy-bottomed saucepan or casserole, toss in the leeks. Season with salt and freshly ground pepper. Cover and sweat over a gentle heat for about 8 minutes or until tender. Add the peppers, toss and add a drop of water if necessary, add half the herbs, cover and continue to cook until the peppers are soft. Add the remaining herbs, season to taste and serve.

VARIATION

Leek, Yellow Pepper & Marjoram Tart Fill a fully baked savoury tart shell with the cooked vegetable mixture and serve immediately. Alternatively, pre-bake tartlet shells, whisk 175ml cream with 2 organic, free-range egg yolks, combine with the leek and pepper mixture, season and fill the tartlets. Bake in the oven at 180°C/gas mark 4 for about 15 minutes.

salads

ROAST RED PEPPER & LENTIL SALAD
with soft goat's cheese

Serves 6

The sweetness of the red peppers complements the goat's cheese and lentils deliciously. A few slices of warm duck breast would be a delicious instead of the goat's cheese here.

225g Puy or Casteluccio lentils

1 carrot

1 onion, stuck with 2 cloves

bouquet garni

extra virgin olive oil

a large handful of finely chopped fresh herbs,
   such as annual marjoram or flat-leaf parsley

freshly squeezed lemon juice

4 red peppers, roasted, peeled, deseeded
   and chopped

a little local goat's cheese, such as St Tola
   or Ardsallagh

sea salt and freshly ground black pepper

lemon wedges and rocket leaves, to garnish

Wash the lentils, put them into a saucepan and cover with cold water. Add the carrot, onion and bouquet garni, bring slowly to the boil. Reduce the heat and simmer very gently for 10–15 minutes, testing regularly. The lentils should be al dente but not hard. Drain, remove and discard the carrot, onion and bouquet garni. Season the lentils while still warm with some extra virgin olive oil, then add some of the herbs and lots of freshly squeezed lemon juice. Season to taste with sea salt and freshly ground pepper.

While the lentils are still warm arrange on a plate or plates, top with freshly roasted red pepper, some slices of goat's cheese, a few rocket leaves and a couple of lemon wedges. Sprinkle with the remaining chopped herbs and serve warm.

APPLE, CELERY & WALNUT SALAD
with spicy chicken

Serves 6

A little twist on the famous Waldorf salad, the spicy chicken perks up the original, but of course can be omitted if you'd rather the original delicious combination.

½ head of celery, cut into 4cm lengths

225g green dessert apples, such as Cox's Orange Pippin or Granny Smith

225g red dessert apples, such as Gala

2 tablespoons freshly squeezed lemon juice

1 teaspoon caster sugar or to taste

150ml homemade mayonnaise (page 146)

50g shelled fresh walnuts, roughly chopped

1 crisp lettuce

sprigs of fresh watercress

freshly chopped flat-leaf parsley, plus extra to garnish

For the spicy chicken

1 tablespoon ground cumin seeds

1 tablespoon paprika

1–1½ teaspoons cayenne pepper

1 tablespoon ground turmeric

1 teaspoon caster sugar

1 teaspoon freshly ground black pepper

2 teaspoons salt

3 garlic cloves, crushed

5 tablespoons freshly squeezed lemon juice

2 organic, free-range chicken breasts

2–3 tablespoons sunflower oil

To make the spicy chicken, mix the cumin, paprika, cayenne, turmeric, sugar, black pepper, salt, garlic and lemon juice in a bowl. Slash the chicken with a sharp knife in a couple of places. Rub the mixture all over the chicken, put in a bowl and cover. Keep in a cool place for at least 3 hours.

Preheat the oven to 180°C/gas mark 4. Put the chicken pieces into a roasting tin with all the paste. Brush or drizzle with the sunflower oil and bake for about 20 minutes then turn over and bake for a further 20–25 minutes depending on the size of the pieces. Baste 2–3 times during cooking. Transfer to a serving dish, spoon the de-greased juices over the chicken and set aside to cool.

Put the celery into a bowl of iced water for 15–30 minutes. Core the apples, cut into 1cm dice. Make a dressing by mixing most of the freshly squeezed lemon juice and caster sugar with 1 tablespoon of mayonnaise (reserve a little lemon juice and caster sugar). Toss the diced apple in the dressing and set aside while you prepare the remaining ingredients.

Add the celery and most of the walnuts to the diced apple with the remaining mayonnaise and chopped parsley, and mix thoroughly. Taste and add more lemon or sugar if necessary. Slice the cold spiced breasts crosswise, toss lightly through the salad.

Put a few crisp lettuce leaves on each plate, pile the salad alongside, add a few sprigs of watercress, scatter the remaining chopped walnuts on top and sprinkle with chopped parsley.

POTATO & SPRING ONION SALAD

Serves 4–6

Everyone insists that potato salad ought to be made with waxy potatoes but I prefer floury Golden Wonders or Kerr's Pinks for superb flavour. Potato salad may be used as a base for other salads and can be bulked out with the addition of cubes of fennel, salami, cooked kabanossi sausage or, most delicious of all, cooked mussels.

1kg freshly cooked potatoes, diced

110ml Ballymaloe French Dressing (page 147)

2 tablespoons freshly chopped chives or
   spring onions

2 tablespoons freshly chopped flat-leaf parsley

110ml homemade mayonnaise (see right)

flaky sea salt and freshly ground black pepper

For the homemade mayonnaise

2 organic, free-range egg yolks

pinch of English mustard powder or ¼ teaspoon
   French mustard

¼ teaspoon salt

2 teaspoons white wine vinegar

225ml sunflower or olive oil or a mixture – I use
   175ml sunflower oil and 50ml olive oil

freshly ground black pepper

To make the mayonnaise, put the egg yolks into a Pyrex bowl with the mustard, salt and white wine vinegar (save the whites to make meringues). Put the oil into a measuring jug with a good pouring spout. Take a whisk in one hand and the oil in the other and drip the oil onto the egg yolks, drop by drop, whisking at the same time. Within a minute you will notice that the mixture is beginning to thicken. When this happens you can add the oil a little faster, but don't get too cheeky or it will suddenly curdle because the egg yolks can only absorb the oil at a certain pace. Taste and add a little more seasoning if necessary.

If the mayonnaise curdles it will suddenly become quite thin, and if left sitting the oil will start to float to the top of the sauce. If this happens you can quite easily rectify the situation by putting another egg yolk or 1–2 tablespoons of boiling water into a clean bowl, then whisk in the curdled mayonnaise, ½ teaspoon at a time until it re-emulsifies. .

The potatoes will have maximum flavour if they are boiled in their jackets and peeled, diced and measured while still hot.

Coat the diced potatoes with Ballymaloe French dressing and mix immediately with chopped chives or onion and parsley. Season well with flaky sea salt and freshly ground pepper. Leave to cool and finally add the mayonnaise. This salad keeps well for about 2 days.

PUY LENTIL, BEAN & whatever you fancy salad

Serves 6

This salad is delicious on its own but can be used as a vehicle to use up loads of other ingredients in your fridge or cupboard – try adding tuna, flaked salmon or smoked mackerel, peppers, chorizo or warm crispy bacon.

50g haricot beans

50g kidney beans

50g Puy lentils

3 small carrots

3 small onions, each stuck with 2 cloves

3 bouquet garni

2 teaspoons freshly chopped parsley

2 teaspoons freshly chopped basil

For the Ballymaloe French dressing

1 finely chopped shallot

250ml extra virgin olive oil

50ml red or white wine vinegar

1 dessertspoon Dijon mustard

1 teaspoon chives, finely chopped

3 large garlic cloves, crushed

1 teaspoon thyme, finely chopped

1 teaspoon flat-leaf parsley, finely chopped

sea salt and freshly ground black pepper

Soak the beans in cold water separately overnight (the lentils do not need to be soaked). Cook the pulses in three separate saucepans, cover each with three cups of cold water and add a carrot, onion and bouquet garni to each pan. Don't salt the beans until almost cooked. Beans take anything from 20 minutes–1 hour to cook, depending on variety and age. Lentils take 15–20 minutes. They should be soft, but still hold their shape. (Keep the cooking liquids – use as a base for a bean or lentil soup, they are full of vitamins and protein.)

Whisk or liquidise the ingredients for the Ballymaloe French dressing together – it should be very well-seasoned and quite sharp.

Make sure the pulses are well drained. While they are still warm, toss the beans and lentils in the French dressing, using enough just to coat the pulses. Season to taste with salt and freshly ground pepper, and fold in the chopped parsley and basil.

A WARM SALAD WITH IRISH BLUE CHEESE

Serves 4

Some ripe, crumbly Cashel Blue cheese now made by Jane and Louis Grubb's daughter Sarah would be wonderful for this salad. A few little cubes of ripe pear are delicious here too. We also love their Crozier Blue cheese.

a selection of organic salad leaves, such as
    watercress, radicchio, endive, rocket, oakleaf
    and butterhead
12 round croutons, 5mm thick, cut from
    a thin sourdough baguette
45g salted butter, softened
1 garlic clove, peeled
140g smoked streaky bacon, cut into 5mm lardons
extra virgin olive oil, for frying
50g Irish farmhouse blue cheese
1 heaped tablespoon of chervil sprigs or freshly
    chopped flat-leaf parsley

For the vinaigrette dressing
1 tablespoon balsamic vinegar
3 tablespoons extra virgin olive oil
2 teaspoons freshly chopped chervil and
    2 teaspoons freshly chopped tarragon or
    4 teaspoons freshly chopped flat-leaf parsley
sea salt and freshly ground black pepper

Preheat the oven to 180°C/gas mark 4.

Whisk together the ingredients for the vinaigrette dressing.

Wash and dry the mixture of salad leaves and tear into bite-sized pieces. Spread both sides of the rounds of bread with softened butter. Put onto a baking tray and bake for about 20 minutes until golden and crisp on both sides. Rub them with a clove of garlic and keep hot in a low oven with the door slightly open. Blanch and refresh the bacon, dry well on kitchen paper. Just before serving, sauté the lardons in a little extra virgin olive oil until golden.

To serve, dress the lettuces with some vinaigrette in a salad bowl. Use just enough to make the leaves glisten. Crumble the cheese with a fork and add it to the salad, tossing them well together. Divide between four plates. Scatter the hot crispy bacon over the top, put three warm croutons on each plate and sprinkle sprigs of chervil or chopped parsley over the salad. Alternatively, arrange the salad on a large serving plate with the croûtons around the edge. Serve immediately with extra vinaigrette in a small bowl.

RED & YELLOW TOMATO SALAD
with mint or basil

Serves 8

A perfect tomato salad is a wonderful thing. In the late summer when we have intensively sweet vine-ripened tomatoes we often serve a tomato salad as a first course. The flavour is so sublime it is a revelation to many people who have forgotten what a tomato should taste like. Tomato salad complements so many other dishes – add some freshly torn mozzarella or burrata and a few basil leaves for a Salad Caprese. A simple tomato salad is wonderful with savoury tarts or quiche or some poached or warm smoked salmon.

8–12 very ripe firm tomatoes
pinch of sugar
Ballymaloe French dressing (page 147)

2–4 teaspoons torn fresh basil leaves or freshly chopped mint
sea salt and freshly ground black pepper

Remove the core from each tomato with the point of a vegetable knife and slice some into 3–4 rounds (around the equator) and others into quarters or random shapes. Arrange in a single layer on a flat plate. Sprinkle with sugar, salt and several grinds of black pepper. Toss immediately in just enough Ballymaloe French dressing to coat the tomatoes, pile them onto a plate and sprinkle with torn basil or chopped mint. Season to taste. Tomatoes must be dressed as soon as they are cut to seal in their flavour.

VARIATION

⌒ *Heirloom Tomato Salad* Use a mixture of vine-ripened heirloom tomatoes in the recipe above and instead of Ballymaloe French dressing I love to use freshly squeezed lemon juice, with best-quality extra virgin olive oil and a little honey.

A WARM SALAD OF IRISH GOAT'S CHEESE
with walnut oil dressing

Serves 4

This is a perfect supper dish, include a few cherry tomatoes or strips of roast red pepper if you want to make it more substantial. It can also be served as a starter or as a cheese course. Walnuts and walnut oil must be fresh, they go rancid and bitter quite quickly so store in a cool place.

a selection of lettuces and salad leaves, such as
    butterhead, frisée, oakleaf, radicchio
    trevisano, rocket, salad burnet,
    golden marjoram
12 x 7.5cm slices toasted small baguette
1 fresh soft goat's cheese, such as Ardsallagh, St.
    Tola or Lough Caum
a little runny honey

16–20 fresh walnut halves
chive or wild garlic flowers or marigold petals
    (*Calendula officinalis*), to garnish
For the walnut oil dressing
6 tablespoons walnut oil or 6 tablespoons
    extra virgin olive oil
2 tablespoons white wine vinegar
dash of Dijon mustard

Wash and dry the salad leaves, tear the larger leaves into bite-sized pieces. Make the walnut oil dressing by whisking all the ingredients together. Cover each piece of toasted French bread with a 2cm slice of goat's cheese. Just before serving, preheat the grill. Place the slices of bread and cheese under the grill for 5–6 minutes or until the cheese is soft and slightly golden.

Meanwhile, toss the salad greens lightly in just enough dressing to make the leaves glisten, drop a small handful onto each plate. Place 3 hot goat's cheese croutons onto each salad, drizzle with honey, scatter with a few walnut pieces and serve immediately. I sprinkle wild garlic, chive flowers or marigold flowers over the salad in season.

A WARM WINTER SALAD WITH DUCK LIVERS
& hazelnut oil dressing

Serves 4

I love this combination of warm livers and perfumed leaves. I am an offal fiend but pretty fussy about sourcing organic.

a mixture of salad leaves, such as Butterhead,
    raddichio, trevisano and oakleaf
6 fresh organic duck or chicken livers
110g carrots
110g celeriac
15g salted butter
12 chicory leaves

sprigs of watercress
sea salt and freshly ground black pepper
1 tablespoon freshly chopped chives, to garnish
For the hazelnut oil dressing
6 tablespoons fresh hazelnut oil
2 tablespoons white wine vinegar (I love Forum
    Chardonnay vinegar)

Wash and dry the salad leaves and tear them into bite-sized pieces. Wash the livers and divide each lobe into two pieces. Dry and keep chilled.

Whisk together the ingredients for the hazelnut oil dressing. Grate the carrot and celeriac on the large part of the grater and toss in about 3 tablespoons of dressing. Season to taste. Toss the salad leaves in a little more of the dressing – just enough to make the leaves glisten.

Melt the butter in a sauté pan, season the livers and cook over a gentle heat for a minute or two, tossing frequently. While the livers are cooking, arrange three leaves of chicory in a star shape on each plate. Put a mound of salad leaves in the centre, tuck in a few sprigs of watercress and top with some celeriac and carrot. Finally, cut the livers in half and while still warm arrange three pieces on each salad. Sprinkle with finely chopped chives to serve.

BEANS GALORE with toasted hazelnuts & coriander

Serves 8

Dried peas, beans and pulses are a brilliant and inexpensive source of protein, particularly important for vegetarians and vegans. In this salad we combine them with freshly cooked French or runner beans. The secret of a super salad is to toss the beans in the well-flavoured dressing while they are still warm. Each has its own particular flavour so experiment with different combinations. Chickpeas are also excellent, and a tahini dressing drizzled over the salad adds a totally different dimension which I love.

110g haricot beans

110g red kidney beans

110g flageolet beans

110g black-eyed beans

4 small carrots

4 small onions

4 bouquet garni

450g French beans

3 teaspoons salt

4 tablespoons Ballymaloe French dressing
   (page 147)

2 tablespoons freshly chopped flat-leaf parsley

2 tablespoons freshly chopped coriander,
   plus extra sprigs to garnish

freshly squeezed lemon juice (optional)

110g toasted hazelnuts, halved

sea salt and freshly ground black pepper

lemon wedges, to garnish

Soak the various types of dried beans separately in cold water overnight.

The next day cover the soaked beans with fresh water, each in a separate saucepan, add a little carrot, onion and bouquet garni to each and cook until just tender. Drain and reserve the cooking water for soup. To cook the French beans, bring 1.1 litres of water to a fast rolling boil, add the salt then toss in the beans. Continue to boil very fast for 5–6 minutes or until just cooked (they should retain a little bite). Drain immediately.

Toss all the beans in the Ballymaloe French dressing while still warm, add the parsley and coriander, season well with sea salt and freshly ground pepper. Taste, sharpen with freshly squeezed lemon juice if it doesn't seem perky enough. Scatter with chopped toasted hazelnuts and coriander sprigs and serve with lemon wedges.

VARIATION

Tahini Sauce There are lots of recipes for this sauce which you can use instead of the Ballymaloe French Dressing. This version is from my brother, Rory O'Connell. Blend 125g tahini paste, 1 crushed garlic clove, a pinch of salt, the juice of ½ organic, unwaxed lemon and 60ml water by hand or in a food processor to achieve a creamy consistency. Add more water and lemon juice as necessary to achieve the correct consistency and acidity level. The sauce should be a slightly thick pouring consistency. Taste and add more salt if necessary.

TRADITIONAL GREEK SALAD
with marinated feta or bocconcini

Serves 6

This salad is served in virtually every taverna in Greece and is delicious when made with really fresh ingredients and eaten immediately. We now make our own feta cheese in our micro dairy, or use Toonsbridge or Ardsallagh feta or our local Knockalara ewe's milk cheese instead of feta, which is seldom in the condition that the Greeks intended by the time it reaches us! I also use Mani olive oil made from the Koroneiki olive. You can also serve this salad in a pitta bread – just split it in half across or lengthways and fill with drained Greek salad and shredded lettuce.

75g cubed feta, Knockalara ewe's milk cheese or whole bocconcini (cut the bocconcini in half if very big)

5 tablespoons extra virgin olive oil

3 tablespoons freshly chopped annual marjoram

½–1 crisp cucumber

1–2 red onions or 6 spring onions

6 very ripe tomatoes

12–18 Kalamata olives

1 tablespoon freshly squeezed lemon juice

salt, freshly ground black pepper and sugar

freshly chopped flat-leaf parsley, to garnish

Cut the cheese into 2.5cm cubes if using feta. Drizzle with 2 tablespoons of extra virgin olive oil and 1 tablespoon of chopped marjoram.

Just before serving, halve the cucumber lengthwise and cut into chunks. Slice the red onions or chop the green and white parts of the spring onions coarsely. Core the tomatoes and cut into wedges. Mix the tomatoes, cucumber, onions, olives and remaining marjoram in a bowl.

Drizzle with the remaining extra virgin olive oil and the freshly squeezed lemon juice. Season with sugar, salt and freshly cracked pepper and toss well. Sprinkle with cubes of feta (or chosen alternative cheese) and sprigs of flat-leaf parsley. Do not toss. Serve at once otherwise it will become watery and tired.

SUMMER GREEN SALAD
with honey & mustard dressing

Serves 4

At Ballymaloe we serve a salad of organic leaves all year round at every lunch and dinner. It varies throughout the seasons depending on what's in the gardens and greenhouse and what wild greens and edible flowers we have access to.

1 mild lettuce, such as butterhead
a selection of the following: finely chopped flat-leaf
    parsley, mint or any herbs of your fancy, spring
    onions, diced cucumber, Mustard and Cress,
    watercress, pea shoots, broad bean tops, Cos,
    radicchio, oakleaf, Chinese leaves, rocket, salad
    burnet, and any other interesting lettuces
    available

For the honey & mustard dressing
150ml olive oil or a mixture of olive and other oils,
    such as sunflower and groundnut
50ml white wine vinegar
2 teaspoons honey
2 heaped teaspoons wholegrain mustard
2 garlic cloves, crushed
sea salt and freshly ground black pepper

To make the honey and mustard dressing, whisk all the ingredients together and whisk well again before use.

Wash and dry the lettuces and other leaves very carefully. Tear into bite-sized pieces and put into a deep salad bowl with the other chosen ingredients. Cover with clingfilm and chill if not to be served immediately.

Just before serving toss with a little dressing – just enough to make the leaves glisten. Serve immediately. Green Salad must not be dressed until just before serving, otherwise it will be tired and unappetising.

VARIATIONS

Summer Green Salad with Edible Flowers Prepare a selection of salad leaves (see above) and add some edible flowers, such as marigold petals, nasturtium flowers, borage flowers, chive flowers or rocket blossoms – one or all of these or some other herb flowers could be added. Toss with a well-flavoured dressing just before serving. This salad could be served as a basis for a starter salad or as an accompanying salad to the main course. Remember to use a little restraint with the flowers!

Farmers' Market Salad with Aged Coolea & Pomegranate Seeds Sprinkle some pomegranate seeds and shavings of aged Coolea cheese over the salad (follow the recipe as above). You can vary the dressings – some pomegranate molasses would be particularly good.

CARROT & APPLE SALAD

with honey & vinegar dressing

Serves 6

This gorgeous little salad can be made in minutes from ingredients you would probably have easily to hand, but shouldn't be prepared more than 30 minutes ahead, as the apple will discolour. Serve either as a starter or as an accompanying salad with glazed ham or pork with crackling (page 78). Choose best-quality wine vinegar and pure unadulterated honey.

225g coarsley grated carrot
285g coarsley grated dessert apple, such as
  Cox's Orange Pippin if available
a few small leaves of lettuce
sea salt and freshly ground black pepper
sprigs of watercress or flat-leaf parsley and wild
  garlic or chive flowers, to garnish

For the honey & vinegar dressing
2 good teaspoons local honey
1 tablespoon white wine vinegar (I use Forum
  Chardonnay vinegar)

Make the dressing by dissolving the honey in the wine vinegar. Mix the coarsely grated carrot and apple together and toss in the dressing. Taste and add a bit more honey or vinegar as required, depending on the sweetness of the apples.

Take six large side plates, white are best for this. Arrange a few tiny leaves on each plate and add the dressed apple and carrot.

Garnish with sprigs of watercress or parsley and sprinkle with wild garlic or chive flowers if you have some. Season to taste.

KINOITH GARDEN SALAD

Serves 4

Visitors to Ireland complain over and over again that it is virtually impossible to get a green salad in a restaurant. It does in fact appear on menus regularly, but when it is served it often includes tomato, cucumber, pepper and sometimes even raw onion rings – not the mixture of lettuce and salad leaves that people had hoped for. I think it's best to keep it simple, serve a well-seasoned dressing made with really good extra virgin olive oil and vinegar and include a few edible flowers and foraged leaves if the fancy takes you.

This is a rather elaborate version which we make in summer from what is in season in the garden. A simple dressing of 3 parts extra virgin olive oil to 1 part wine vinegar, seasoned with a little salt and freshly ground pepper, makes a splendid dressing. Choose a really good extra virgin olive oil such as Capezzana, Fontodi or Selvapiana.

a selection of fresh lettuces, salad leaves and
    edible flowers, such as butterhead, oakleaf,
    pea shoots, saladisi, lollo rosso, radicchio,
    frisée, mizuna, purslane, red orach, rocket,
    edible chrysanthemum leaves, wild sorrel
    leaves or buckler leaf sorrel, chervil, golden
    marjoram, salad burnet, borage, courgette
    or squash blossoms, sage flowers, nasturtium
    flowers and tiny leaves, marigold petals, chive or
    wild garlic flowers, herb leaves, such as lemon
    balm, mint, flat-leaf parsley, chervil, lovage, tiny
    sprigs of tarragon, dill or annual marjoram

For the dressing
4 tablespoons extra virgin olive oil
1 tablespoon white wine vinegar (I use Forum
    Chardonnay vinegar)
1 teaspoon local honey
1 teaspoon grainy mustard
1 garlic clove, crushed
flaky sea salt and freshly ground black pepper

Whisk all the dressing ingredients together, store in a screw-top jar and shake again to re-emulsify if not serving immediately.

Just before serving, drizzle some dressing over the leaves in a large, deep bowl, just enough to make the leaves glisten. Toss gently until the leaves are nicely coated. Sprinkle a few more edible flowers over the top.

desserts

ALMOND TART or tartlets with raspberries

Serves 12/
Makes 24 tartlets
or 2 tarts

This is a little gem. The tartlets are also delicious with just a spoonful of raspberry jam and a blob of cream. Try to use shallow tartlet tins and you'll need the best quality ground almonds you can find.

110g soft butter

100g caster sugar

110g ground almonds

lemon balm or rose geranium leaves (*Pelargonium graveolens*), to garnish

For the redcurrant glaze

350g redcurrant jelly

1 tablespoon lemon juice or water (optional)

For the filling

whichever ripe fruit is in season, such as
fresh raspberries or loganberries, halved
strawberries, redcurrants, blackcurrants,
poached rhubarb or sliced fresh peaches
or nectarines, peeled and pipped grapes
or blueberries

300ml whipped cream

Preheat the oven to 180°C/gas mark 4.

Cream the butter, add the sugar and ground almonds but don't overbeat. Put a teaspoon of the mixture into 24 patty tins or divide the mixture between two 18cm sandwich tins. Bake for 20–30 minutes or until golden brown. The tarts or tartlets will be too soft to turn out immediately, so cool for about 5 minutes before removing from the tins. Do not allow to set hard or the butter will solidify and they will stick to the tins. If this happens, pop the tins back into the oven for a few minutes so the butter melts and then they will slide out easily. Leave to cool on a wire rack.

To make the redcurrant glaze, melt the redcurrant jelly in a small stainless steel saucepan and add the liquid if necessary. Stir gently, but do not whisk or it will become cloudy. Cook it for just 1–2 minutes or the jelly will darken. Store any leftover glaze in an airtight jar and reheat gently to melt it before use. The quantities given above make a generous 300ml glaze.

Just before serving, arrange the raspberries, loganberries or other selection of fruit on the base. Glaze with redcurrant jelly. Decorate with rosettes of whipped cream and garnish with tiny lemon balm or rose geranium leaves.

ORANGE MOUSSE with dark chocolate wafers

Serves 6–8

This mousse sounds slightly 'retro' now, but everyone loves it when we serve it on the sweet trolley at Ballymaloe House. Be careful to measure the gelatine accurately.

2 oranges (1½ if very large)
4 organic, free-range eggs
70g caster sugar
3 tablespoons water
2 teaspoons gelatine
1 organic, unwaxed lemon
225ml whipped cream

For the chocolate wafers
50g best-quality dark chocolate

To decorate
2 oranges
225ml whipped cream
a pinch of caster sugar

Wash and dry the oranges; grate the rind on the finest part of a stainless steel grater. Put into a bowl with 2 eggs, 2 egg yolks and the caster sugar. Whisk to a thick mousse, preferably with an electric mixer. Put the water in a little bowl, measure the gelatine carefully and sprinkle over the water. Leave for a few minutes until the gelatine has soaked up the water and feels spongy to the touch. Put the bowl into a saucepan of simmering water and allow the gelatine to dissolve completely. All the granules will dissolve and it should look perfectly clear.

Meanwhile, squeeze the juice from the 2 oranges and 1 lemon, measure and if necessary bring up to 300ml with more orange juice. Stir a little into the gelatine and then mix well with the remaining juice. Gently stir this into the mousse; cool in the fridge, stirring regularly. When the mousse is just beginning to set around the edges, fold in the softly whipped cream. Whisk the 2 egg whites stiffly and fold in gently. Pour into a glass bowl or into individual bowls. Cover and leave to set for 3–4 hours in the fridge or better still overnight.

Meanwhile, make the chocolate wafers. Melt the chocolate in a bowl over barely simmering water. Stir until quite smooth. Drizzle on a non-stick baking mat or a heavy baking tray. Put into a cold place until stiff enough to cut into square or diamond shapes.

While the chocolate is setting, make the orange-flavoured cream. Grate the rind from an orange, add half into the whipped cream and add a pinch of caster sugar to taste. Peel and segment the oranges. Decorate the top of the mousse with orange segments and pipe on some rosettes of orange-flavoured cream. Sprinkle with a little of the grated orange rind. Peel the chocolate wafers off the mat and use them to decorate the edges of the mousse.

CARAMEL MOUSSE WITH PRALINE

Serves 6

A light and rich mousse, caramel and praline is a very special combination of flavours.

225g granulated sugar

100ml cold water, plus 2 tablespoons

150ml boiling water

4 organic, free-range egg yolks

2 teaspoons gelatine

300ml whipped cream

For the praline

25g granulated sugar

25g whole almonds, unskinned

Put the granulated sugar and 100ml cold water into a heavy-bottomed saucepan. Stir over a gentle heat until the sugar is dissolved and the water comes to the boil. Continue to boil without stirring until it turns a rich chestnut-brown colour. Remove from the heat and immediately add the boiling water. Return to a low heat and cook for 4–6 minutes until the caramel thickens to a thick, syrupy texture. The cooking time depends on the size of the saucepan and the heat.

Meanwhile, whisk the egg yolks until fluffy, then pour the boiling caramel onto the egg yolks, whisking all the time until the mixture reaches the ribbon stage or will hold a figure of eight shape. Sponge the gelatine in the 2 tablespoons of water in a small bowl. Put the bowl into a saucepan of simmering water until the gelatine has completely dissolved. Stir a few spoonfuls of the mousse into the gelatine, then carefully add the mixture to the rest of the mousse. Fold in the whipped cream gently and pour into six individual serving dishes or one larger serving dish. Cover and chill until set.

To make the praline, put the sugar into a small heavy-bottomed saucepan over a low heat, sprinkle the whole almonds on top in a single layer. Do not stir. Gradually the sugar will melt and turn to caramel. When this happens, and not before, rotate the saucepan so that the caramel coats the almonds. By now the almonds should be popping. Turn onto a non-stick baking mat or into a lightly oiled tin. Leave to cool completely and become hard and then crush to a coarse powder. Decorate the mousse with a quenelle of cream and some crushed praline.

VARIATION

Caramel Soufflé Fold in 2 stiffly beaten egg whites after the cream. Chill until set and decorate as before.

SUMMER PUDDING

Serves 12–16

Summer Pudding bursting with soft fruit and served with lots of softly whipped cream is one of the very best puddings of the year. I actually make Summer Pudding with cake, a sort of Marie Antoinette version, but many people line the bowl with slices of white bread instead. I've used a mixture of fruit here, but it is also delicious made with blackcurrants alone. Summer Fruit Salad with Rose Geranium (page 168) also makes a successful filling, but you need to cook the blackcurrants and redcurrants until they burst and then add the soft fruit. Remember to pour the fruit and syrup while boiling hot into the sponge-lined bowl, otherwise the syrup won't soak through the sponge properly.

2 x 18cm sponge cakes
6–8 large sweet geranium leaves (*Pelargonium graveolens*)
600g granulated sugar
700ml cold water

225g blackcurrants, strings removed
225g redcurrants, strings removed
450g raspberries or 225g raspberries and 225g strawberries
softly whipped cream, to serve

Cut each round of sponge in half, horizontally. Line a 1.7-litre pudding bowl with the cake, crusty side inwards. It doesn't matter if it looks quite patched, it will blend later.

Put the rose geranium leaves, sugar and cold water into a saucepan. Bring to the boil for 2 minutes, add the blackcurrants and redcurrants and cook for 3–4 minutes until the fruit bursts. Remove from the heat then add the raspberries (and strawberries). Immediately, ladle some of the hot liquid and fruit into the sponge-lined bowl (on a plate to catch overflow later). When about half full, if you have scraps of cake put them in the centre. Then fill to the top with fruit. Cover with a final layer of sponge. Put a plate on top and press down with a heavy weight. Leave to cool completely. Store in the fridge for a minimum of 24 hours before serving, but it will keep for 5–6 days.

To serve, unmould onto a deep serving dish and pour any leftover fruit and syrup over the top and around the sides. Serve with lashings of softly whipped cream.

CHOCOLATE MERINGUE GATEAU

Serves 6

This recipe makes two layers of meringue but you can double the ingredients for a celebration cake or to make individual little meringues.

2 organic, free-range egg whites
125g icing sugar
2 rounded teaspoons cocoa powder
(I use Valrhona)

For the chocolate & rum cream
30g best-quality dark chocolate
15g unsweetened chocolate
1 tablespoon Jamaican rum
1 tablespoon double cream
300ml softly whipped cream
For the chocolate wafers
55g best-quality dark chocolate

Preheat the oven to 150°C/gas mark 2.

Mark 2 x 19cm circles on parchment paper. Check that the bowl is dry, spotlessly clean and free of grease. Put the egg whites into the bowl and add 110g sieved icing sugar all at once; whisk for about 10 minutes until the mixture forms stiff, dry peaks. Sift together the cocoa and the remaining 15g sieved icing sugar and fold in very gently. Spread into circles with a palette knife and bake immediately in the oven for 45 minutes or until just crisp. Leave to cool completely then peel off the paper.

Meanwhile, very gently melt the chocolate with the rum and 1 tablespoon of cream, or in a bowl over simmering water. Cool and add 2 tablespoons of whipped cream into the chocolate. Mix well, then fold that into the remaining softly whipped cream; don't stir too much or it may curdle.

To make the chocolate wafers, melt the chocolate in a bowl over barely simmering water. Stir until quite smooth. Spread on a non-stick baking mat or heavy baking tray. Put into a cold place until stiff enough to cut into square or diamond shapes.

Sandwich the two meringue discs together with most of the chocolate and rum cream and add rosettes on top. Decorate with the chocolate wafers and a sprinkling of cocoa.

BLACKCURRANT FOOL

Serves 6

We all love fools, super easy to make, you can use a variety of fruit from rhubarb to green gooseberries. Raspberries and strawberries make a delicious fool too, but don't need to be cooked first.

350g fresh or frozen blackcurrants
200ml stock syrup (see right)
600ml very softly whipped cream

For the stock syrup
175 granulated sugar
300ml water

To make the stick syrup, dissolve the sugar in thewater and bring to the boil. Boil for 2 minutes then leave it to cool. Store in the fridge until needed.

Cover the blackcurrants with 200ml stock syrup. Bring to the boil and cook for about 4–5 minutes until the fruit bursts. Liquidise and sieve or purée the fruit and syrup. When the purée has cooled, add the softly whipped cream. Frozen blackcurrants tend to be less sweet. Taste – you may need to add extra sugar. A little stiffly beaten egg white may be added to lighten the fool. The fool should not be very stiff, more like the texture of softly whipped cream. If it is too stiff, stir in a little whole milk rather than more cream. Serve with shortbread biscuits.

Alternatively layer the purée and softly whipped cream in tall sundae glasses, ending with a drizzle of thin purée over the top.

VARIATIONS

Blackcurrant Ice Cream Leftover fool (when made with cream alone), may be frozen to make delicious ice cream. Serve with coulis made by thinning the blackcurrant purée with a little more water or stock syrup.

Blackcurrant Popsicles Add a little more syrup and dilute with extra water if necessary. It needs to taste sweeter than you would like because the freezing dulls the sweetness. Pour into popsicle moulds, cover, insert a stick and freeze until needed. Best eaten within a few days.

BALLYMALOE VANILLA ICE CREAM

Serves 12–16

Surprise, surprise, really good cream makes really good ice cream. The Ballymaloe ice creams are made on an egg-mousse base with softly whipped cream. It produces a deliciously rich ice cream with a smooth texture that does not need further whisking during the freezing period. This ice cream should not be served frozen hard; remove it from the freezer at least 10 minutes before serving. Other flavourings can be added to the basic recipe: liquid ingredients such as melted chocolate or coffee should be folded into the mousse before adding the cream. For chunkier ingredients such as chocolate chips or muscatel raisins soaked in rum or Pedro Ximénez, dates or prunes, finish the ice cream, semi-freeze it and then stir them through, otherwise they will sink to the bottom.

4 organic, free-range egg yolks
100g granulated sugar
200ml cold water

seeds from ⅓ vanilla pod or 1 teaspoon
    pure vanilla extract
1.2 litres softly whipped cream (measured
    after it is whipped, for accuracy)

Put the egg yolks into a bowl and whisk until light and fluffy (keep the whites for meringues). Combine the sugar with the cold water in a small heavy-bottomed saucepan. Stir over a low heat until the sugar is completely dissolved, then remove the spoon and boil the syrup until it reaches the 'thread' stage, about 106–113°C: it will look thick and syrupy, and when a metal spoon is dipped in the last drops of syrup will form thin threads. Pour this boiling syrup in a steady stream onto the egg yolks, whisking all the time by hand. (If you are whisking the mousse in a food mixer, remove the bowl and whisk the boiling syrup in by hand; otherwise it will solidify on the sides of the bowl.)

Add the vanilla seeds or vanilla extract and continue to whisk the mixture until it fluffs up into a thick, creamy white mousse.

This is the stage at which, if you're deviating from this recipe, you can add liquid flavourings such as coffee. Fold the softly whipped cream into the mousse, pour into a bowl, cover and freeze.

VARIATION

⌐ *Vanilla Ice Cream with Pedro Ximénez Raisins* Warm the Pedro Ximénez or rum. Pour over the raisins and allow to plump up and macerate then add to the ice cream. Drizzle a little Pedro Ximénez over the ice cream on the plate just before you tuck in.

174   ⁓ desserts

MERINGUE NESTS with strawberries & cream

Serves 6

I no longer use strawberries or raspberries out of season, as they, particularly strawberries, have zero flavour and get quite the supplement of pesticides and herbicides. There are many good things to fill these meringue nests with – blackcurrants, poached kumquats, rhubarb, *fraises du bois…*

2 organic, free-range egg whites
125g icing sugar
fresh mint or lemon balm leaves, to garnish

For the filling
225g small strawberries in season
225ml whipped cream

Preheat the oven to 150°C/gas mark 2. Cover a baking tray with parchment paper. Draw out 4 x 9cm circles on the paper or mark them with the tip of a knife on the flour. Put the egg whites and icing sugar into a spotlessly clean bowl and whisk until the mixture forms stiff peaks. This can take 8–10 minutes in an electric mixer. Alternatively, you can whisk it by hand but it takes quite a long time, so if you have even a hand-held mixer it will speed up matters a lot.

Put the meringue mixture into a piping bag with a number 5 rosette nozzle. Pipe a few blobs onto each circle and spread thinly with a palette knife. The meringue should not be more than 5mm thick. Then carefully pipe a wall of meringue rosettes around the edge of each circle. Bake for 45 minutes or until the meringue nests will lift easily off the paper. Turn off the oven and leave the meringues to cool in the oven.

To assemble, remove the stalks from the strawberries and cut them into slices lengthways. Pipe some whipped cream into each nest and arrange the slices of strawberries on top. Decorate with tiny rosettes of whipped cream and garnish with fresh mint or lemon balm leaves.

VARIATIONS

⌐ *Meringue Nests with Autumn Raspberries & Pistachios* Substitute raspberries for strawberries, scatter with chopped pistachio nuts and garnish with fresh mint leaves.

⌐ *Meringue Nests with Lemon Curd* Substitute homemade lemon curd for strawberries and garnish with fresh mint leaves.

SUMMER FRUIT SALAD with rose geranium

Serves 8–10

Rose geranium (*Pelargonium graveolens*) and many other varieties of scented geraniums are ever present on our windowsills here at Ballymaloe. We use the delicious lemon-scented leaves in all sorts of ways. Occasionally we use the pretty purple flowers as well to enliven and add magic to otherwise simple dishes. The crystallised leaves, all frosty and crinkly are wonderful with fresh cream cheese and fat, juicy blackberries. I discovered this recipe, which has now become a perennial favourite, quite by accident a few summers ago as I raced to make a pudding in a hurry with the ingredients I had to hand.

110g raspberries
110g loganberries
110g redcurrants
110g blackcurrants
110g small strawberries
110g blueberries
110g *fraises du bois* or wild strawberries
110g blackberries

For the syrup
450ml cold water
325g granulated sugar
6–8 large rose geranium leaves, plus extra
   to garnish

Put all the freshly picked berries into a white china or glass bowl. Put the cold water, sugar and sweet geranium leaves into a stainless steel saucepan and bring slowly to the boil, stirring until the sugar dissolves. Boil for just 2 minutes. Cool for 10–15 minutes or more then pour the syrup over the fruit and set aside to macerate for several hours, if time allows.

Remove the geranium leaves. Serve chilled, with softly-whipped cream or vanilla ice cream (page 176) or alone. Garnish with a few fresh sweet geranium leaves.

VARIATION

Winter Fruit Salad with Sweet Geranium Leaves Follow the recipe above but substitute best-quality frozen berries and currants. Pour the boiling syrup over the berries in the bowl. This will defrost the fruit and cool the syrup at the same time.

CRÈME CARAMEL with caramel shards

Serves 6

A timeless dessert that is exquisite when carefully made – serve chilled.

For the custard
600ml whole milk
vanilla pod or ½ teaspoon pure vanilla
    extract (optional)
4 organic, free-range eggs
40g caster sugar

For the caramel
200g granulated sugar
110ml water
For the caramel sauce
60ml water
For the caramel shards
110–150g granulated sugar

Preheat the oven to 150°C/gas mark 2. Put the cold milk into a saucepan and add the vanilla pod (if using). Bring to just under boiling point. Leave to cool and infuse for 10–15 minutes. Whether you are using a vanilla pod or vanilla extract, the milk must be brought to just under boiling point first. Whisk the eggs, caster sugar and vanilla until thoroughly mixed but not too fluffy.

Meanwhile, make the caramel. Put the sugar and water into a heavy-bottomed saucepan and stir over a gentle heat until the sugar is fully dissolved. Bring to the boil, remove the spoon and cook until the caramel becomes dark golden brown or what we term chestnut colour. Do not stir and do not shake the pan. When the caramel is ready for lining the moulds, it must be used immediately or it will become hard and cold. Coat the bottom of 6 x 7.5cm soufflé dishes or cups with the hot caramel. Dilute the remaining caramel with the 60ml water, return to the heat to dissolve and set aside.

Pour the slightly cooled milk onto the egg mixture, whisking gently as you pour. Strain and pour into the prepared moulds, filling them to the top.

Place the moulds in a bain-marie of simmering water, cover with a sheet of parchment and bake for about 35 minutes. Test the custard by putting a skewer in the centre, it will come out clean when the custard is fully cooked.

Meanwhile, to make the caramel shards, boil the sugar and water to the caramel stage – chestnut colour, cool slighty, spoon onto an oiled baking tray or onto silicone paper. When cold and crisp, use to decorate the crème caramels. Alternatively, put either granulated or caster sugar into a low-sided stainless steel saucepan. Stir continuously over a medium heat until the sugar melts and caramelises. When it has almost reached the 'chestnut' stage, remove from the heat and leave to stand for a few minutes. Then spoon into shapes as above.

Cool the caramels and turn out onto individual plates, pour the caramel sauce around the edge. Decorate with caramel shards.

COUNTRY RHUBARB CAKE

Serves 8

This traditional rhubarb cake, based on an enriched bread dough, was made all over Ireland and is a treasured memory from my childhood. It would have originally been baked in the bastible or 'baker' over the open fire. My mother, who taught me this recipe, varied the filling with the seasons – first rhubarb, then gooseberries and later in the autumn, apples and plums.

340g plain flour, plus extra for dusting
pinch of salt
½ teaspoon bicarbonate of soda (bread soda)
55g caster sugar, plus extra for sprinkling
85g butter
1 organic, free-range egg

165ml whole milk, buttermilk or sour milk
680g rhubarb, finely chopped
170–225g granulated sugar
beaten organic, free-range egg, to glaze
softly whipped cream and soft brown sugar,
  to serve

Preheat the oven to 180°C/gas mark 4.

Sift the flour, salt, bicarbonate of soda and caster sugar into a bowl and rub in the butter. Whisk the egg and mix with the milk, buttermilk or sour milk. Make a well in the centre of the dry ingredients. Pour in most of the liquid and mix to a soft dough; add the remaining liquid if necessary.

Sprinkle a little flour on the work surface. Turn out the soft dough and pat gently into a round. Divide into two pieces: one should be slightly larger than the other; keep the larger one for the lid.

Dip your fingers in flour. Roll out the smaller piece of pastry to fit a 25cm enamel or Pyrex pie plate. Scatter the rhubarb all over the base and sprinkle with the granulated sugar. Brush the edges of the pastry with beaten egg. Roll out the other piece of dough until it is exactly the size to cover the plate, lift it on and press the edges gently to seal them. Don't worry if you have to patch the soft dough. Make a hole in the centre for the steam to escape. Brush again with beaten egg and sprinkle with a very small amount of caster sugar.

Bake for 45 minutes–1 hour or until the rhubarb is soft and the crust is golden. Leave it to sit for 10–15 minutes before serving so that the juice can soak into the crust. Sprinkle with caster sugar. Serve still warm, with a bowl of softly whipped cream and some moist, brown sugar.

BALLYMALOE COFFEE ICE CREAM
with Irish coffee sauce

Serves 6–8

This ice cream is so good, you may be surprised that I am using instant coffee, but believe me it works brilliantly here – liquid espresso will result in little splinters of ice. It will keep for months in the freezer but is much more fresh-tasting when eaten within a couple of days of being made.

For the coffee ice cream
2 organic, free-range egg yolks
50g granulated sugar
110ml water
½ teaspoon vanilla extract
3 teaspoons instant coffee
½ teaspoons boiling water
600ml whipped cream

For the Irish coffee sauce
175g granulated sugar
75ml water
225ml strong coffee or espresso
1 tablespoon Irish whiskey

Put the egg yolks into a bowl and whisk until light and fluffy. Put the sugar and the water into a small, heavy-bottomed saucepan over a low heat. Stir until all the sugar is dissolved and then remove the spoon and do not stir again until the syrup reaches the thread stage, 106–113°C. It will look thick and syrupy; when a metal spoon is dipped in, the last drops of syrup will form thin threads. Pour this boiling syrup in a steady stream onto the egg yolks, whisking all the time. Continue to whisk until it fluffs up to a light mousse which will hold a figure of eight. Stir in the vanilla extract. Mix the instant coffee with just ½ teaspoon of boiling water, in a little bowl. Add some mousse to the paste and then fold the two together. Carefully fold in the softly whipped cream. Pour into a stainless steel or plastic bowl, cover and freeze.

To make the Irish coffee sauce, put the sugar and the water into a heavy-bottomed saucepan over a medium heat, stir until the sugar dissolves and the water comes to the boil. Remove the spoon and do not stir again until the syrup turns a pale golden caramel. Then add the coffee and return to the heat to dissolve. Leave to cool and add the whiskey. This sauce keeps brilliantly for 2–3 months and doesn't need to be refrigerated.

To serve, scoop the ice cream into a serving bowl or ice bowl. Pour the sauce over the top.

GREEN GOOSEBERRY COMPOTE with elderflowers

Serves 6–8

When I'm driving through country lanes in late May or early June, I suddenly spy the elderflower blossoms in the hedgerows. I know then it's time to go and search on gooseberry bushes for the first hard, green fruit, far too under-ripe at that stage to eat raw, but wonderful cooked in tarts or fools or in this delicious compote. Elderflowers have an extraordinary affinity with green gooseberries and by a happy arrangement of nature they are both in season at the same time.

900g green gooseberries
2–3 elderflower heads
400g granulated sugar

600ml cold water
elderflowers, to decorate
elderflower cream, to serve

First top and tail the gooseberries. Tie the elderflower heads in a little square of muslin (alternatively, just add them whole and fish them out later), put in a stainless steel or enamelled saucepan, add the sugar and cover with the cold water. Bring slowly to the boil and continue to boil for 2 minutes. Add the gooseberries and simmer just until the fruit bursts. (The tart green gooseberries must actually burst otherwise the compote of fruit will be too bitter.) Leave to cool completely.

Serve in a pretty bowl and decorate with fresh elderflowers. Serve with elderflower cream (whipped cream flavoured with elderflower cordial).

VARIATION

Green Gooseberry & Elderflower Fool Liquidise the compote, mix with softly whipped cream to taste – about half volume of whipped cream to fruit purée. Serve chilled with shortbread biscuits.

APPLE CHARLOTTE

Serves 4–6

This is the scrummiest, most wickedly rich apple pudding ever. A friend, Peter Lamb, makes it as a special treat for me every now and then. It's also a brilliant and delicious way to use up bread and apples. I make my Apple Charlotte from old varieties of eating apples – my favourites are Egremont Russet, Charles Ross, Cox's Orange Pippin or Pitmaston Pineapple. It's sinfully rich but gorgeous.

225g butter

1kg dessert apples

2–3 tablespoons water

175g caster sugar, plus extra to dust

2 organic, free-range egg yolks

good-quality white yeast bread

Preheat the oven to 200°C/gas mark 6.

To make the clarified butter, melt the butter gently in a saucepan or in the oven. Allow it to stand for a few minutes, and then spoon the crusty white layer of salt particles off the top of the melted butter. Underneath this crust there is clear liquid butter, which is the clarified butter. The milky liquid at the bottom can be discarded or used in a white sauce. Clarified butter is excellent for cooking because it can withstand a higher temperature when the salt and milk particles are removed. It will keep covered in the fridge for several weeks.

Peel and core the apples. Melt a little of the clarified butter in a stainless steel saucepan, chop the apples into cubes and add to the saucepan with a couple of tablespoons of water and the sugar. Cover and cook over a gentle heat until the apples break into a thick pulp. Beat in the egg yolks one by one – this helps to enrich and thicken the apple purée. Taste and add a little more sugar if necessary.

Melt the remaining clarified butter and use a little of this to brush the inside of a 13 x 20cm loaf tin then dust it with caster sugar. Cut the crusts off the bread and cut into strips about 4cm wide and 13cm high and quickly brush them with the clarified butter. Line the sides of the tin with butter-soaked bread. Cut another strip to fit tightly into the base of the tin. Brush it on both sides with butter and tuck it in tightly. Fill the centre with the apple pulp. Cut another strip of bread to fit the top. Brush with melted butter on both sides and fit it neatly to cover the purée.

Bake for 20 minutes then reduce the heat to 180°C/gas mark 4 for a further 15 minutes or until the bread is crisp and a rich golden colour.

To serve, run a knife around the edges in case the bread has stuck to the tin. Invert the Apple Charlotte onto a warm oval serving plate. It won't look like a thing of beauty, it may collapse a bit, but it will taste wonderful. Serve with lots of softly whipped cream.

LEMON FLUFF with limoncello cream

Serves 4–6

This is a gorgeous old-fashioned family pudding which separates into two quite distinct layers when it cooks; it has a lovely fluffy top and a creamy lemon base, provided it is not overcooked.

40g butter

225g caster sugar

3 organic, free-range eggs

75g plain flour

2 organic, unwaxed lemons

300ml whole milk

icing sugar, to decorate

300ml softly whipped cream flavoured with
    Limoncello, or crème fraiche, to serve

Preheat the oven to 180°C/gas mark 4.

Cream the butter until really soft, then add the caster sugar and beat well. Separate the egg yolks and whisk in one by one, then stir in the flour. Grate the rind of 2 lemons on the finest part of the grater. Squeeze and strain the juice and add the rind and juice then add the milk.

Whisk the egg whites stiffly in a bowl and fold gently into the lemon mixture. Pour into a 1.2-litre pie dish, place in a bain-marie and bake for 35–40 minutes. Dredge with icing sugar.

Serve immediately alongside thesoftly whipped cream flavoured to taste with Limoncello, or some crème fraiche.

ACKNOWLEDGEMENTS

I've been so touched by the many people for whom the *Simply Delicious* cookbooks hold a special memory.

Those who bring me well-worn, gravy splattered copies to sign. This book is for all of you who requested a reprint. I've chosen my 100 favourite recipes from *Simply Delicious 1, 2, Fish* and *Vegetables* – what a tough choice that was and such a revelation that so many recipes have stood the test of time and are still simply delicious.

Special thanks to Joanna Copestick for commissioning this collection and my editor Vicky Orchard for keeping me in check, no easy matter….To photographer, Pete Cassidy for the beautiful photos and food stylist Lizzie Harris and prop stylist Agathe Gits for cooking and styling my food so beautifully.

Rosalie Dunne, my heroic PA of 24 years, came out of retirement to type the manuscript. Can you imagine that I still write all my books in longhand 29 years later? Thank you Rosalie.

Special thanks also to Tim and all my extended family of children, grandchildren and once again to the recently deceased Myrtle Allen – my lifelong inspiration.